Media and Democracy

MEDIA AND DEMOCRACY

Edited by

Nirmala Rao Khadpekar

2012

Icfai Books
The Icfai University Press

Media and Democracy

Editor: Nirmala Rao Khadpekar

First Edition: 2012
Printed in India

Published by

This book is published by IUP.
University Campus, Agartala-Simna Road,
P.O. Kamalghat Sadar, Agartala – 799210, Tripura (West)
E-mail: info@iupindia.org
Website: www.books.iupindia.org

ISBN: 978-81-314-2728-6

Contents

Overview

This book looks at the historic relationship between media and democracy and how this relationship has gone a long way in nurturing or warping democratic growth of countries. The book tries to establish that the content provided by the media forms opinion. The way media works in certain countries is examined to enable the formation of an opinion on the subject. There is an increasing susceptibility of manipulation at work from inter and intra-governmental authorities or by economic forces. Often, democracy is practised without accountability, which provides the convenient illusion of popular consent. This, in actuality, is the power of the state and privileged interests, which are being consolidated with willing media support. There is too much emphasis on the business aspect than on survival issues, and the role of the Fourth Estate keeps getting diminished of purpose. The social debate is increasingly missing; the equilibrium in society needs real issues like public health and environment to be discussed and pursued. It is almost as if, now, media needs to be democratized, which is a bit of a contrary thing to say. The book examines whether the media is losing its democratic moorings and whether the media itself needs a large dose of democratization to do its work well. Democracy needs a lot of maintenance and media is its formidable ally in the digital age.

The first article is titled "**Media's Mandate in a Democracy**" by the editor of this book, *Nirmala Rao Khadpekar,* who explains that the essentially participative nature of democracy makes communication dependant. That is how media becomes the tool of choice for disseminating the good work required to nurture democracy. This becomes more important in new democracies and older democracies that need to be revitalized and protected. The electorate and the institutions of power and authority are impacted by the way media conducts itself and provides all the necessary information to citizens to facilitate informed decision-making and help participate in the democratic process. Following on from print, broadcast, Internet, and popular FM radio now, have taken over the airwaves with the advantage of voice and view, it is possible to have deep impact on the audience. They have also impacted newspaper shape, size, look, feel and content. The rich diet of political ideas is slowly disintegrating into sensationalism and voyeurism in almost sinister manner by the powers vested in fewer and fewer elitist groups. Money powers begets influence and influence multiplies money, and the public duties are forgotten. Media has begun the dangerous activity of 'sleeping with the enemy'.

The second paper, "**Building Our Media: Community Broadcasting, Social Movements and Media Democratization**" by *Robert A Hackett* and *William K Carroll*, is sourced from the Global Media Journal. The article examines how both ideologically and historically the expansion of communication rights have given rise to counter hegemonic movements to contest social order and the dominant means of public communication. The authors argue that, in effect, media democratization is the institutional organization of public communication, so as to enable all groups and sectors in society to place ideas and elements of culture into general circulation, and to participate in constructing public cultural truth. They see community broadcasting as an important pillar of a broader, and increasing global process – that of media democratization – seeing it as a part and parcel of building 'communicative democracy'. In actuality this process comprises efforts to change media messages, practices, institutions and contexts including state and international policies towards enhancing participation and equality, and helps enable a social order that nurtures the autonomy and development of people within it. The paper also looks critically at democratic deficits in the media realm, social movement theory and democratic activism, emerging civil society based media reforms, and community media and democratic media activism.

The third article is an essay titled "**Democracy, Development, Peace and Communication: An Overview of their Roles and Interaction**" by *Dov Shinar* of the Global Media Journal. The discussion is about how communication has been recognized as a crucial factor in the peace-democracy-development triangle with the media's role being examined with the ethical normative approach, the professional approach and the structural approach. There is a discernable gap between mainstream 'official speak', consumer oriented media and credible communication, which cried out for a more democratic media structure including older and newer technologies. Given the fact that, at present, a few transnational media corporations in more developed countries dominate the commercial media system, a more mixed media system is recommended to provide better service. Production of peace, democracy, development contents and the socialization of journalists and audiences is discussed in the light of Africa, the Middle East, Northern Ireland, and Eastern Europe. Strategies for increasing the effectiveness of peace-oriented, democratic and development-conscious media are outlined and examined along with the conscious efforts being made to harness media into promotion of peace and furthering the establishment of democracies which are in the interest of the people.

IV

The fourth article titled "**Structural and Social Forces Restricting Media News Content in Democracies: A Critical Perspective**" by *Gregg A Payne*, from Scientific Journals International offers a critical perspective of the news product generated by the US media. It argues that the social and structural conditions dictating content in the US are similar to those effecting media artifacts of authoritarian political regimes. Media is seen under both political conditions to be tools of elite interests preoccupied with ideological control of social, political, and economic environments. The contention is that in both democratic and authoritarian political circumstances, the news product are homogenized, offering little by way of divergent perspectives. The consequent information deprivation that ensues is linked to an impoverished public discourse that is antithetical of the democratic process. Events and topics need to be infused with ideological perspectives to provide diversity and contribute vigorously to creating a free marketplace of ideas rather than homogenizing it to naturalize a distorted reality by perpetuating myths and narratives serving elite interests.

The fifth article titled "**Media in New Democracies: Agents for Change or Beneficiaries of Change**" by *Sallie Hughes* is a book review. The book, 'Negotiating Democracy: Media Transformations in Emerging Democracies', edited by *Isaac A Blankson* and *Patrick D Murphy*, is important also because it informs about countries that do not normally get included in the US-based Academic Press, which is the information the rest of the world feeds on. The purpose of the book is to assess the relationship between media and democracy within the broader framework of globalization regarding economic liberalism. An important point is made about how neoliberalism appears to link international actors more seamlessly than political and economic flows under colonialism or the Cold War. It informs the readers about various individual media systems in new and emerging democracies and how they contend with transitions from authoritarian rule in a global environment favoring economic liberalization. With the terms of reference established on geopolitical history of media and globalization, it also looks at electoral democracy on media ownership and content, and media interaction with discourses on democratic rights and practices.

The sixth paper titled "**Democracy in the Media Society: Changing Media Structures – Changing Political Communication?**" by *Jens Lucht* and *Linards Udris* examines how more and more attempts are being made to draw readers away from traditional newspapers and increasing legal and financial pressures on public service broadcasting lowers the quality of programming. Even more mergers of big media organizations with capital (and media power) are becoming concentrated in a few hands, with growing importance of 'free dailies' distributed in big European cities which tabloidize news structures and deconstruct them homogeneously. The argument is for a research design that connects the structural and content side of the media, presenting indicators and their operationalization and conduct content analysis of political communication across countries and over time to link the indicators. The essential findings show that in Western style democracies, the Press has disentangled itself from their former social and political ties to a mode of increasing commercialization leading to a diffusion of 'media logics' into political communication and its further media dissemination as a whole.

"**Media and Judicial Activism**" is an article written by *Shikha Singh*, in which the connection between the Judiciary and the Media is examined in the light of public activism. They feel it is their duty to take up the cudgels against something wrong in the society. The judiciary sometimes takes cues from media investigations and sets up a Public Interest Litigation and sometimes, the media takes a bit off a judgment and goes to town with a PIL of its own. Increasingly, judicial activism is coming on the radar of public life, and though we tend to celebrate it, it is really a symptom of a deep malaise in society. The problems are when either the judiciary or the media force their 'liberal' views on society to steer the action in a particular direction. And when they do it together they can do immense societal good or harm. The article looks at the issues involved in a media judiciary connection; and how adverse court orders do not become activism, nor does a media campaign always become activism.

"e-Democracy in Australia: The Challenge of Evolving a Successful Model", by *Jenny Backhouse*, drawn from the Electronic Journal of e-Government, discusses the current status of e-democracy initiatives in Australia. It considers factors that might contribute to the evolution of a successful model in the Australian context. In particular, it examines whether the analogies can be drawn from the world of e-business, which has transitioned from an over-hyped boom and then bust in the early years into a steadier and sustained growth in more recent times. Politicians have feedback on public sentiments through issues taken up by the media via public polling by media outlets and other media organizations. There is concern about falling memberships of political parties and trade unions and young people not registering to vote. But citizen apathy issues are complex to gauge as voting is compulsory in Australia, yet claims of political disengagement of the populace are discussed in the media with concerns about deepening the already evident digital divide. E-journals like *Online Opinion* provide a forum of discussion for social and political issues and encourage pertinent research like a recent government health enquiry that subsequently realized visibility in the mainstream media.

The situation in Canada is explored in **"Democracy of, in and through Communication: Struggles Around Public Service in Canada in the First Half of the Twentieth Century"** by *Patricia Mazepa*. In reviewing the application of public service principles in the Press, telecommunications and radio historically, the paper tracks develop alternatives that address limitations in state and commercially provided public services across a wide range of communication and cultural packages. The paper uses published and archival sources to identify examples of Canadian history that understand service as facilitating the making of communication and culture using the political economy of culture approach resulting in adopting a different view of public service. It provides a historical and reflexive view on public service in Canada across media and suggests that public service principles need to be grounded in democracy of, in and through communication as a potential guide to policy decision-making. The paper finds that the concept of public service has been restricted to thinking in a sender-receiver based model based consumption and applied accordingly to different media, which has limited potential in democratic communication.

Taken from a new democratic country, Bhutan, is the paper titled **"Media in the New Political Order"** by *Dorji Wangchuk* of the Centre for Bhutan Studies. Bhutan has been undergoing fundamental changes in politics, economy, social fabric, and every other aspect as a nation. In the new political environment mass media will play a vital role in sustaining the democracy. The special part of the Bhutan story is that the path to democracy has been forged by none other than the Monarch himself. The author feels that the success of the new path will depend a lot on how the media is managed and practiced in the country. Whether the provisions of the draft constitution which guarantees freedom of speech, Press and expression, will be translated into 'spirit' by the government regulation and people's exercising them. The paper looks at the development of the modern mass media in Bhutan and the role it has played in the overall modernization process and what is expected from it in the future. The paper attempts to engage with issues of press freedom, need for own media model, and the role of public service and the independent press in the changing political scenario.

The last article titled **"Media Use in Estonia: Trends and Patterns"** by *Peeter Vihalemm,* sourced from Nordicom gives an overview of general trends in media use in Estonia over the last 15 years, making some comparisons with Nordic countries. The changes in the media landscape since the beginning of the post communist transformation in Estonia from 1991 are traced and declared as substantial. There are some commonalities with many European countries regarding the impact of the emerging new media and global TV while other transformations are specific features of a transition to a market economy and a democratic political order. A completely new and diversified media system has emerged as also a new pattern of media use among audiences as habits and expectations change has been rapid and radical. Besides discussing general trends, the article gives insights into some audience-related aspects of changes, more specifically about age and ethnicity.

1

Media's Mandate in a Democracy

Nirmala Rao Khadpekar

The electorate and the institutions of power and authority are impacted by the way media conduct themselves and provide all necessary information to citizens to facilitate informed decision-making take part in the democratic process. Since the nature of democracy is essentially participative, media becomes the tool of choice for disseminating the good work required to nurture democracy. This connection becomes more important in new democracies and also for older democracies that need to be revitalized and protected. The article examines whether the media is losing its democratic moorings. Democracy without accountability creates an illusion of popular consent which is the worst of all. Democracy needs a lot of maintenance and media is its formidable ally in the digital age.

Introduction

It is widely believed by political and social scientists that Media plays a vital and defining role in a Democracy due to its essentially participative nature. Media would include any agency, modern or traditional, that operates for the expression and propagation of ideas and information, usually with intent to influence or control the electorate or the institutions of power and authority. Over time, the concept of a free press was extended to the broadcast media, and later to the internet, with a series of democratic responsibilities and obligations to serve the public. The mass media in a democratic society need to provide all the necessary information for citizens to facilitate their informed decision-making and participation in the democratic process. It is critical that the information provided by mass media be objective, indepth and prompt to create vigorous debate on issues of common concern, thus enabling citizens to be knowledgeable and participate intelligently in public affairs. As media cross fertilizes ideas, it has a major role in democratizing countries as democracy requires informed citizens to make informed political choices when they elect their representatives.

Many newspersons today are steeped in market logic[1] and prefer to conform for convenience in a time where consumerism is more desired than active citizenship. Democracy without answerability builds a false impression of popular sanction while increasing the governmental power and that of the moneybags. The social debate is increasingly missing; the equilibrium in society needs real issues like public health and environment to be discussed and pursued. The Internet sites, blogs, webcasts and other new media outlets jostle for capturing attention and creation of impact in a 'marketplace of ideas that consolidates, or diversifies depending on held perspectives'.[2] Media's role is not a single focus one though it deals with basic freedoms which need to adapt to current philosophy and policy developments. Media has a multifaceted role as an integral part of democratic society, but also needs to be practiced as a profit making enterprise. Take that as a given but it does appear as if almost, now media needs to be democratized. When mainstream media sidelines the reality of suffering, say like it is said to have done in Darfur, mechanisms like MySpace can take over and see that the story reaches scores of more people. They did this with a video called 'Footage from Sudan and Chad', where visuals and facts were put out with George Clooney (whose father Nick Clooney was a journalist) featuring in it. The use of blog and podcasts were effectively used to cover the media's apparent unease with the story. Kevin Scott has discussed this requirement in *Pressethic: Democratizing*

1 *www.thirdworldtraveler.com/Media_control_propaganda/*

2 *www.bu.edu/com/mediatoday/*

the Media where he shows how technology has given access not only to the wherewithal of using media, and journalists have to be open themselves to multiple media platforms to be versatile enough to deliver on developing platforms with expertise and knowledge to get the attention of viewer, listeners and readers, in whichever order of choice as required.

Malnutrition of (Political News) Diet

The need for a well informed public fed on a rich diet of political news, seems to be becoming a casualty in the new conglomerate culture. The current problems hinge on whether the media's accountability to their corporate owners, whose mandate is to manufacture news as consumer commodities, is affecting their role to be a means to empower morally responsible citizens. Due to the spectacular media realignments[3] in the recent past, smaller numbers have power over the main media dissemination and publishing houses. The democratic rights and responsibilities are being usurped by powerful corporate and political interests for partisan ends. However, mass media in all countries are becoming increasingly susceptible to manipulation, either by governmental authorities or by economic forces. It has become hard to protect and forecast the future policies of countries due to the conflicting opinions about media globalization. "On the one hand, the World Trade Organization (WTO) promotes the international free trade of audiovisual services. On the other side there are other organizations, like the United Nations Educational, Scientific and Cultural Organization (UNESCO), which combat these attempts," says Manfred Kops in his paper – *More media, less democracy*.[4] The smaller countries stand to jeopardize their national culture and identity by the international free trade pursued by the unbridled broadcast of international programs sought by commercialization of the international broadcasting markets. The special rights and protections that are granted to media by citizens and their governments to enable them to be free from fettles are increasingly coming under scrutiny to check whether they deserve this unique status anymore as the bias issues and explosive nature of new media technologies needs a kind of restraint that is not much visible.[5] The rich diet of political ideas has been slowly diminishing to sensationalism and voyeurism in almost sinister

3 *http://money.cnn.com/2007/05/14/news/companies/media_mergers/*

4 2008 InfoChange India News & Features

5 *www.streamingmedia.com/west/program/*

manner by the powers vested in fewer and fewer elitist groups. Money power begets influence, and influence multiplies money, public duties are forgotten. Holding the authorities accountable for crimes, corruption and incompetence is what a democracy's wheels are oiled on appearing to be slowly diminishing. In fact, media appears to be indulging in the dangerous activity, to use a phrase from the espionage and military intelligence field, of 'sleeping with the enemy'. The propaganda approach to media coverage is thoroughly discussed in Noam Chomsky's works, notably in 'Manufacturing Consent' where he argues that choices of story and volume and quality of coverage are experiencing huge and pre planned dichotomization in the handling of 'inconvenient materials (placement, tone, context, fullness of treatment) in ways that serve political ends.'[6]

Loud Call

The electorate and the institutions of power and authority are impacted by the way media conduct themselves to provide all necessary information to citizens to facilitate informed decision-making and participate in the democratic process. Press freedom appears to be practiced more in its abuse than it should be put to find the truth. The clamour for limitations on media independence and liberty has come to pass based on increasing concerns about national security and skepticism whether media outlets augment autonomous governance and community involvement. The Centre for Democracy and Governance in Washington whose directive is to encourage the changeover to and firming up of democratic rule across the world has produced many technical papers to emphasize the importance of the role of media. They say good 'information is essential to the health of democracy for ensuring that citizens make responsible, informed choices rather than acting out of ignorance or misinformation; and, information serves a "checking function" by ensuring that elected representatives uphold their oaths of office and carry out the wishes of those who elected them.' When there is a face off type of relationship between the media and government as happens sometimes in most societies, it represents 'a vital and healthy element of fully functioning democracies'.

---

6 Manufacturing Consent, Noam Chomsky

Participatory Nature

Jonathan Jones[7] has discussed a successful engagement with citizens in a democracy, citing the anti SEZ movement. Common people who stand to lose their livelihoods have been at the centre of this movement in parts of Goa and Bengal (Singur and Nandigram). They are supported by political parties, non governmental organizations and external social activists. The media says the author has had a free hand to cover the SEZ issue and publish their observations widely on front pages and with indepth stories about agitations. The important function of dispersing information about the issues at stake in the anti SEZ were disseminated across India informing people about issues and showing them how to agitate. The media in India has received kudos for covering SEZ issues with its related land scam issues and is doing a great democratic service which is quite vital to the political and economic future of India. The good democratic work needs to continue in developing countries, but the concentration needs to be on substantive issues that require communication support.

Development strategies have to come from the societies that need to implement them and not be externally imposed as conditions. When the essence of the debate emanates from the people who thereby 'own' them, the product will not have the flavor of processes foisted on society by the aid giving organizations who decide what needs to be prioritized. Then the leaders of these people will become accountable to the citizens rather than the aid givers. Poverty reduction strategies in particular need to be understood well to enable their debate and scrutiny by an enabled media. The Millennium Development Goals of 2000 have recognized that development strategies simply have to be owned 'by' the elected governments of countries. Since the citizens of the countries depend on a capable media to interpret policy in a way that citizens, especially those living below the poverty line can comprehend for scrutiny and debate. The citizens need to be able to hold the governments to account on how public monies are being allocated and spent. According to James Deane in his paper, Democracy, Development and the Media,[8] 'the poorer the people are, the more they need such information.' And it is the media which arms them with mechanisms to build capacities to articulate

---

7 India's Democracy has a Heartbeat, Seminar.

8 *www.communicationforsocialchange.org/mazi-articles*

their opinions and develop perspectives on important issues like public spending, ostensibly on their behalf. Though it is necessary to create a media sector that supports democracy, legal reform institutions need to be developed alongside to sustain the media sector to yield long-term results in short period of time and to sustain for the future. Some form of self regulation by media will need to be in place to develop a powerful approach for better media development in a democracy, for a democracy, by a democracy. With proper focus on ownership and accountability the jewels of participation and empowerment need to be taken forward to focusing on ownership and accountability through a rights based approach.

Conclusion

A new commitment to openness is required to affirm the connection between media and democracy in de-regulated regimes. Media in a democracy manifests in different ways in different countries. An enabling environment for truth in communication which encourages broader political debate which can hold governments accountable is what the ideal situation is. Such a situation needs work and sustenance of freedom from bias and lobbies which means if you have it, it is a task to maintain it that way. The issues that shape the lives of citizens are provided by media information dissemination; for debate from people to develop and communicate their perspectives from and through the media. Most journalists have energetically, over time, described their reason for existence as being telling the truth as it is, to empower people with knowledge and arm them with information they can use for their own betterment. In poorer societies, if they do not have this democratic media, having anything else which is ostensibly working in their names is a farce. The countries of the Africas, Iran, Bhutan, and the countries of Scandinavia to name a few have vibrant ways of framing the contexts for news/information dissemination. The wave of democratization or the huge wish of people in developing countries to have a say in their uplift should be a great load on journalists across various media. While young and new democracies need to be nurtured, the older democracies need to be revitalized and protected. Media does appear to be losing its democratic moorings and whether the media itself needs a large dose of democratization to do its work well, needs to be addressed. Democracy needs a lot of maintenance, for which media is a formidable ally, especially in the digital age. Liberalization of broadcast media has its advantages; it engages people heretofore out of reach into the public arena, making information more and more accessible to include more and more people. New technologies have via the internet freed people to respond at once and air their views in response. Unless the media reinforces their role of holding governments to account and facilitating knowledgeable public debate, enlightened development strategies will be demoralized just like they used to be in bad old times. Democracies will remain in name, media with a reputation and people without a voice. An intensive approach for media in development and livelihood issues can build on the issues of civic affairs, habitat, environment and cultural identities, to name a few. A democratic and democratized media has a long way to go.

(Nirmala Rao Khadpekar is a Senior Faculty Member and Coordinator, at Icfai Research Centre, Ahmedabad. She can be reached at nirmala.khadpekar @gmail.com).

2

Building Our Media
Community Broadcasting, Social Movements and Media Democratization

Robert A Hackett and William K Carroll

This article sees community broadcasting as an important pillar of a broader, and increasing global process – that of media democratization – seeing it as a part and parcel of building 'communicative democracy'. How both ideological and historical expansion of communication rights has given rise to counter hegemonic movements to contest social order as the dominant means of public communication is also examined. Democratic deficits in the media realm, social movement theory and democratic activism, emerging civil society based media reform coalitions, and community media and democratic media activism are discussed. Effectively media democratization is the institutional organization of public communication to enable all groups and sectors in society to place ideas and elements of culture into general circulation, and to participate in constructing public cultural truth.

Source: http://stc.uws.edu.au/gmjau/index.html, Global Media Journal, Australian Edition, Volume 1/1 2008.

Community broadcasting can be seen as an important pillar of a broader, and increasingly global, process – that of media democratization. What do we mean by that term? Media democratization comprises efforts to change media messages, practices, institutions and contexts, including State and international communications policies, in a direction that enhances participation and equality, and helps to enable a social order that nurtures the autonomy and development of all people within it (Hackett & Carroll 2006, 88). Put differently, media democratization is part and parcel of building "communicative democracy", the institutional organization of public communication, so as to enable all groups and sectors in society to place ideas and elements of culture into general circulation, and to participate in constructing public cultural truth (Jakubowicz, 1993; White, 1995).

Both ideologically and historically, the expansion of communication rights has often been a by-product of the energies of social movements that seek to tell the suppressed stories of the people, and advance their interests (Traber, 1993). Historically, counter-hegemonic movements have built radical media that contest not only the social order but also, implicitly at least, the dominant means of public communication (Downing *et al*, 2001). In recent decades, and particularly the past several years, such radical media have been joined by media reform advocacy groups that consciously seek not only to use communications media to pursue their primary political goals, but rather, directly and explicitly, to transform the media system as such.

Such movements are responding to regimes that deny popular communication rights, and thereby inhibit the prospects of success for progressive social movements. Such repression is most obvious in the case of dictatorships that deny people the freedom to express their opinions. But even in the Anglo-American North Atlantic heartland of neo-liberal globalization and, (rather debatably), political democracy, there is a massive 'democratic deficit' in public communication, with a number of dimensions. According to Hackett and Carroll (2006, Chap. 1) these include:

- the media system's failure to constitute a democratically adequate public sphere;

- centralization of political and symbolic power inherent in the political economy of media industries;
- media's complicity in maintaining inequality through exclusions of culture and class that include the 'digital divide';
- media's role in homogenizing social viewpoints – narrowing the diversity of public discourses;
- media's failure to help sustain healthy communities and political cultures, due to factors ranging from insufficient localism and excessive national chauvinism, to commercially-driven audience fragmentation and content trivialization;
- media's participation in the corporate enclosure of knowledge through expansion of 'intellectual property rights';
- elitist processes of communication policy-making, which exclude the public from shaping mandates of the cultural industries;
- erosion of privacy, and the increase in surveillance and censorship, in electronic space since the events of 9/11, 2001.

Is the Democratic Deficit Lethal?

Around the world, the negative consequences of undemocratic media abound. Sometimes it is not too much to say that media justice is a matter of life and death. Most obviously, consider the role of radio in facilitating and co-ordinating the genocide and 'ethnic cleansing' in Rwanda and the former Yugoslavia in the 1990s. Even in the US, a country with a formal constitutional commitment to freedom of the press, undemocratic media can have lethal consequences. Many critics hold the US news media partly responsible for the ability of the Bush administration to sway public opinion in favour of the 2003 invasion of Iraq, with all its disastrous consequences. American media failed critically to examine key administration claims about Saddam Hussein's alleged weapons of mass destruction or his implied connection to al Qaeda and the 9/11 terrorist attacks, often even amplifying these dubious claims. Conversely, media underplayed counter-balancing themes such as previous British and American support for Saddam's regime, alternative ways of deposing him without war, and Iraqi civilian casualties resulting from years of UN sanctions and from the invasion itself (for example see Kellner, 2005, 63-100; Solomon & Erhlich, 2003).

What accounts for these patterns of coverage? Consider the layers or levels of factors that influence the production of news (Shoemaker & Reese, 1995). At every level, powerful influences pushed American journalism towards a propagandistic role before the Iraq war: the ideological and professional assumptions of news workers themselves; daily routines that embody dependence on official sources (and "embeddedness" with the troops); the organizational needs of media corporations (such as the pursuit of profits and ratings); extra-media factors (such as an institutional complex that makes corporate media natural allies of US militarism and capitalist globalization); and ideology and culture (currently hegemonic myths of the American nation and its experience of war) (Hackett, 2004; McChesney, 2002).

Does it matter how the dominant media framed the Iraq crisis, or whether they looked for contexts and realities beyond official claims? Public opinion research suggests that ordinary Americans do not lightly approve of war, but rather that six 'screens' need to be passed before they will support military interventions: a rogue leader or regime; evidence tying them to heinous crimes or imminent threat; the exhaustion of non-military means; military allies to share the risks; a visionary objective (such as liberation or peace); and early non-military intervention (Kay, 2000, cited in Lynch & McGoldrick, 2005, 97). In light of that model published before the fateful year of 2001, the dominant US news media helped to create perceptions that pushed public opinion through those screens.

The lethal consequences of the democratic deficit are not limited to genocide and war on such a terrifying scale. Consider the role of media stereotyping in reinforcing everyday racism. Malkia Cyril and her colleagues at the Oakland-based Youth Media Council have argued that the continual media representation of young black males as criminals makes it easier for police to shoot unarmed African Americans with impunity.

Quite apart from war and hate propaganda, media concentration can have deadly, if unintended, side effects. Following the 1996 Telecommunications Act which allowed a few large companies to buy up an unprecedented number of local stations, corporate rationalization and cost-cutting led to drastic reductions in local programming. Eric Klinenburg (2007, 6-7) tells the story of one of the consequences. In Minot, North Dakota, on January 18, 2002, a freight train derailment released a toxic cloud of 240,000 gallons of anhydrous ammonia. Terrified citizens tuned in to radio KCJB AM910, the designated emergency broadcaster, for directions on how to stay safe. But instead they discovered:

> ...KCJB, and every other radio station in town, were not reporting any news or information about the anhydrous spill. Instead, all six of Minot's name-brand stations...continued playing a standard menu of canned music, served up by smooth-talking DJs trading in light banter and off-color jokes while the giant toxic cloud floated into town. Although the broadcasts originated in Minot, every one of the town's commercial stations was owned and operated by the San Antonio-based conglomerate Clear Channel Communications, which acquired the outlets in 2000 and replaced locally produced news, music and talk programs with prepackaged content engineered in remote studios and transmitted to North Dakota through digital voice-tracking systems. Clear Channel consolidated operations for its Minot stations into two central offices, neither of which had a live staff member interrupt the regularly scheduled automated shows to issue an alert immediately after the spill.

People didn't know to avoid going outdoors, or driving through the toxic cloud. The result: one death, seventeen injuries, 330 immediate health problems, and over a thousand more during the next month, out of a population of 37,000. Perhaps local emergency response planners should have been better prepared, but radio industry concentration, and its "Wal-martization" of local communities, were integral to this deadly picture.

Upon consideration, the lethal democratic deficits noted above can be seen as failures by dominant media to help build sustainable and just communities. The town of Minot lacked reliable local radio. Rwanda's Tutsi community and African-Americans in the US, lacked a sufficient voice to defend their communities from the promotion of hatred in mass media. Rwanda itself apparently lacked consensus-building national media. And the community of global opposition to the Iraq war could not counter the domestic power of America's war propaganda machine.

Good News

The good news, as noted above, is that even in the heartland of global capitalism, there is an emergent movement to democratize media. Organized networking and advocacy to change the structures or practices of media, and/or the rules of media governance, is occurring at local, national and transnational levels. Such activism takes a variety of strategic routes encapsulated by the slogan of Vancouver's annual Media Democracy Day: "Know the media, change the media, be the media". Knowing the media implies media education, understood broadly, from developing curricular materials for schools (like the British Columbia Association for Media Education), undertaking satirical exposes of mass-mediated consumerism (AdBusters magazine), or conducting research on press coverage of public issues (NewsWatch Canada).

"Being the media" refers to independent, alternative or citizens' media, which have illuminated the history of democratic movements and resistance to oppression (Downing *et al,* 2001), and which can help to counterbalance the media's democratic deficit (and its lethal consequences). As a transnational network of community media, Our Media is arguably a force for this kind of media democratization, and in the display tables at Vancouver's Media Democracy Day, citizens' media have always been well represented.

Changing the media can include "strategic communication" on the part of citizens' groups in efforts to shift the frames and content of dominant media. It also includes struggles within the belly of the beast, as media workers' unions seek to protect what they can of journalists' professional autonomy, and sometimes develop policy proposals for more democratic media (like the year-long exercise by Canada's Communications, Energy and Paperworkers Union to develop a policy manual, For Democratic Canadian Media). At its most ambitious level, changing the media entails tackling the state and its regulatory agencies, which set the rules that shape who owns and controls media, who has access, what subsidies and support they receive, what kind of content and usages are most likely to dominate the media, given the incentive structure that policy creates. Rewriting the rules is the project of media reform, and that will only move in a progressive direction on the backs of a broad coalition, spearheaded by groups focusing on policy reform. Fortunately, these are emerging in the North Atlantic heartland, including Britain's longstanding Campaign for Press and Broadcasting Freedom, Free Press formed in the US in 2002, and most recently, Canada's Campaign for Democratic Media (*www.democraticmedia.ca*).

Civil society-based media reform coalitions are emerging at the international level as well. One example is the Campaign for Communication Rights in the Information Society, or CRIS. Several activist researchers connected with CRIS have identified key principles and policies that need forceful articulation within the emerging system of global media governance, currently dominated by the contradictory and often destructive logic of neoliberalism. These are:

- Strengthen public access to information; combat enclosures of the public domain that are imposed by restrictive so-called "intellectual property right" regimes;
- Set technical standards for the internet to make them more friendly to the needs of developing countries;
- Limit concentration of global media ownership;
- Support public service and community media, both within and between nations and cultures;
- Regulate telecommunications to provide universal service, and 'network neutrality' (fair access to content and service providers);
- Support freedom of expression, but also recognize legitimate limitations on it, such as incitement to hate and genocide (O Siochru, Girard & Mahon 2002, 176-79).

Social Movement Theory and Democratic Media Activism (DMA)

Media democratization is not going to occur as a 'natural' byproduct of dominant social logics. To the contrary, media democratization constitutes a challenge to the centralization of political power in the hands of states, whether old-style authoritarian governments, or the emerging "market authoritarian" regimes needed to enforce the global patterns of inequality, exclusion, expropriation, exploitation and coercion associated with neoliberalism. Moreover, the full realization of media democratization entails an "enabling environment" that extends well beyond the media field, to include also a supportive legal framework, a redistribution of material and symbolic resources, and a culture that privileges values of respect and participation (Zhao & Hackett, 2005). For all these reasons and more, the democratization of communication can be regarded as "a social movement process" (White, 1995). At their best, social movements embed some of the practices of democratic communication, but in addition, the scale of transformation needed to actualize "communicative democracy" (Jakubowicz, 1993) on a society-wide basis necessitates the mobilization of movement energies. Thus, it would be useful to consider the recent emergence of media reform coalitions and democratic media activism (DMA) in light of social movement theory, complemented by Pierre Bourdieu's field theory. Does DMA constitute a nascent movement in its own right? What does theory suggest about DMA's prospects for political success and about the role of community broadcasting in relation to it?

We cannot address those questions fully here. Instead, we draw from a recent book on "the struggle to democratize public communication" in order to highlight some of the most pertinent arguments (Hackett & Carroll 2006).[1]

Social movement theory and an analysis of the institutional fields within which DMA intervenes (i.e., the media, and national and international politics), suggest some distinctive characteristics of DMA:

- Resource Mobilization Theory highlights that DMA has an especially strong 'free rider' problem. That is, the effort to achieve democratic media falls disproportionately on specialized individuals and groups, but the benefits are widely dispersed. The incentive facing communities and movements that would benefit from democratic media, is to let others do the work of achieving them. But of course, if everybody does that, there would be no activism, no movement.
- DMA arises partly out of the asymmetrical relationship between dominant media and movements; movements are more dependent on the media than vice versa (Gamson & Wolfsfeld, 1993). In their efforts to win more discursive space for their own struggles, each movement potentially improves

the conditions of access to the public sphere for other progressive movements. But more than most movements, DMA will face a publicity blockade from the media institutions that it critiques.

- Our case studies, and much other research and practice, strongly suggest that DMA emerges in large part from broader political and social waves – especially the communicative needs and political struggles of subaltern groups and communities, and critical social movements – such as organized labour in the UK, and racialized minorities in the US.

Using Pierre Bourdieu's technique of field analysis, we consider that DMA is attempting to intervene in the field of media, as a relatively autonomous institutional sphere with its own logics, agent-positions, and forms of capital (resources) for which they compete. The media field (within 'advanced' national states) has characteristics that help condition the nature of DMA:

- high capacity to intrude on the functioning of other fields (such as politics and the economy);
- vulnerability to influence from the political and economic fields, even structured subordination to them;
- boundaries that are porous and ill-defined: consider the difficulty of defining who is a journalist, as blogs and citizens' journalism emerge on the internet, and as the traditional providers of mainstream journalism, media corporations, either abandon investment in primary newsgathering, or transform their news content into commercialized infotainment.

What are some of the implications of the above points, extracted from much broader traditions in social theory?

- The weakness of media/journalism's autonomy from state and capital puts severe limits on the strategy of reform from within, in the absence of strong allies from without. The strategic importance of media to the legitimation, publicity and marketing needs of corporations and states, means that effective media reform campaigns are likely to provoke hostile reaction.
- At the same time, struggles against the power of capital and/or state on non-media fronts, will often overlap with the 'contestation of media power'

(Couldry, 2003); a media democracy project has beneficiaries, and potential allies, outside the media field.

- The specificity of the media field suggests the need to develop capacities and strategies suited to mobilizing constituencies, in ways that enable media power to be challenged. The media field creates many potential beneficiaries for media democratization, but only some groups have been drawn into DMA.
- DMA lacks a clear collective identity, given its largely secondary nature as a by-product of other movements, and its low issue salience. It is a 'process issue' that does not threaten material interests strongly and directly enough to inspire an 'old-style' movement like organized labour. Nor does it often evoke identities as distinct from, nor as deep as, other so-called new social movements. Many people self-identify as environmentalists or feminists or gays/lesbians; few activists identify themselves primarily as media democrats.
- Crucially, DMA is less likely to constitute a movement in itself than a nexus between movements.

Community Media and Democratic Media Activism

The points sketched above suggest several reasons for regarding community-based and participatory media, run by and for the communities they are intended to serve, as having an especially important role in the broad and global struggle to achieve popular and democratic media.

1. *Connection to Social Movements.* History shows that popular, radical and community media, as well as media activism, are connected to broader social and political currents, particularly social movements, and cycles of protest (Downing *et al,* 2001). Community media often function, if not as the voice of other social movements, then in sympathetic engagement with them. One thinks of Co-op Radio in Vancouver, which has programs empowering distinct communities from Palestinians and union workers, to gay, lesbian and transgendered people. There are also programs on the environment and current affairs from a progressive perspective. Our research found that a particularly important vector of media democratization – evident in the history of San Francisco's Media Alliance and other groups – runs from such subaltern communities, to media training or media

production (including community broadcasting), to interventions that challenge dominant media structures and policies (Hackett & Carroll, 2006, 109). Community media are an important potential link between media activism, and broader social movements.

2. *Incentives.* Community media would benefit directly from the kinds of reforms proposed by progressive media policy advocacy. At both the national and transnational levels, media reformers like CRIS, call for legal recognition and material support for community and public service media as a way to enhance communication rights. That is not to deny that there are potential tensions between priorizing tax-supported state-owned public broadcasters versus community broadcasters, or between the citizen-journalists of community media and salaried journalists in the corporate press. Such tensions require an expansive and 'big tent' vision for media democratization; no single type of media can serve all democratic purposes, and a fully democratic communication system requires structured pluralism (Curran, 2000). Generally speaking, media reform would bring benefits to the values and communities that community media serve. Thus, of all the potential beneficiaries of media reform, community media and their constituencies are at the forefront.

3. *Lowering the "costs of mobilization".* Community media are particularly well-placed to overcome or bypass some of the barriers that full-fledged media democratization movements face. As noted above, corporate and state media are hardly likely to lend publicity to a movement that challenges their own legitimacy and power. That suggests an important role for community media in 'conscientizing' their constituencies about communication rights and media reform. DMA's 'free rider' problem also means that it typically relies upon volunteer activists and faces the challenge of long-term sustainability. Here too, community media organizations can help, to the extent that they have institutionalized resources – paid staff, networks, associations (like AMARC, the global association of community broadcasters); constituencies, audiences, and supporters or employees who have essential movement-building skills, in strategic communication, research, media production, journalism and/or political lobbying. Community media's resources may appear minuscule next to global corporate behemoths like Rupert Murdoch's News International, but they are much greater

than those available to many other social movements. The old adage remains true: organized money can only be beaten by organized people, and community media have resources essential to such collective mobilization.

4. *Sense of Identity.* As a movement-nexus built around shifting issues and coalitions, media democratization doesn't necessarily need the same kind of identity-based solidarity as other movements. But our research suggests that alternative and community media are precisely the sites where DMA comes closest to acquiring a collective sense of belonging to a movement.

We do not mean to suggest that community media should "lend a hand" to democratic media activism, as if it were a form of charitable donation. Rather, community media are already integrally part of a broader and growing process of media democratization. It is a matter of identifying and building upon the synergies and common ground in that broader, and potentially world-transformative, process.

(Robert A Hackett is a PhD, Political Studies, School of Communication, Simon Fraser University. He can be reached at hackett@sfu.ca

William K Carroll is a Professor in department of Sociology, University of Victoria. He can be reached at wcarroll@uvic.ca).

References

Couldry, Nick. (2003) 'Beyond the hall of mirrors? Some theoretical reflections on the global contestation of media power,' in•N. Couldry and J. Curran (eds) *Contesting Media Power: Alternative Media in a Networked World.* Lanham: Rowman & Littlefield: 39-54.

Curran, James. (2000) 'Rethinking Media and Democracy,' in J. Curran and M. Gurevitch (eds) *Mass Media and Society*, 3rd edn, London: Arnold: 120-155.

Downing, John D.H. with Ford, T. V., Gil, G. and Stein, L. (2001) *Radical Media: Rebellious Communication and Social Movements,* Thousand Oaks: Sage.

Gamson, William A. and Wolfsfeld, Gadi.(1993) 'Movements and Media as Interacting Systems', *Annals of the American Academy of Political and Social Science,* 528:114-25.

Hackett, Robert. (2004). "Drumbeating for War? Media versus Peace and Democracy," in George Melnyk (ed), *Canada and the New American Empire.* Calgary: University of Calgary Press.

Hackett, Robert A. and Carroll, William K. (2006). *Remaking Media: The Struggle to Democratize Public Communication*, London: Routledge.

Jakubowicz, Karol (1993) 'Stuck in a groove: Why the 1960s approach to communication democratization will no longer do,' in Slavko Splichal and Janet Wasko (eds) *Communication and Democracy*. Norwood: Ablex: 33-54.

Kay, Alan F. (2000). "When Americans Favor the Use of Force," *International Journal of Public Opinion Research* 12 (2)(Summer): 182-90.

Kellner, Doug (2005). *Media Spectacle and the Crisis of Democracy*. Boulder & London: Paradigm.

Klinenberg, Eric (2007). *Fighting for Air: The Battle to Control America's Media*. New York: Metropolitan Books.

Lynch, Jake and McGoldrick, Annabel. (2005). *Peace Journalism*. UK: Hawthorn Press.

McChesney, Robert W. (2002). "September 11 and the Structural Limitations of US Journalism," in Barbie Zelizer and Stuart Allan (eds), *Journalism after September 11*. London and New York: Routledge, pp. 91-100.

O Siochru, Sean, Girard, Bruce and Mahan, Amy. (2002) *Global Media Governance: A Beginner's Guide,* Lanham, Boulder, New York, Oxford: Rowman & Littlefield.

Solomon, Norman and Erlich, Reese. (2003) *Target Iraq: What the News Media Didn't Tell You.* New York: Context Books.

Traber, Michael. (1993) 'Changes of communication needs and rights in social revolutions,' in S. Splichal and J. Wasko (eds) *Communication and Democracy*, Norwood, NJ: Ablex: 19-31.

White, Robert A. (1995) 'Democratization of communication as a social movement process,' in P. Lee (ed.) *The Democratization of Communication*, Cardiff: University of Wales Press: 92-113.

Zhao, Yuezhi and Hackett, Robert A. (2005) 'Media globalization, media democratization: challenges, issues, and paradoxes', in R.A. Hackett and Y. Zhao (eds) *Democratizing Global Media,* New York: Rowman & Littlefield: 1-33.

3

Democracy, Development, Peace and Communication: An Overview of their Roles and Interaction

Dov Shinar

The communication deficit that was evident at the beginning of the 21st century between democracy and development is discussed in the light of the growth of democratic media spaces in many parts of the world to balance between private and public social interests. The media's role is examined with the ethical normative approach, the professional approach and the structural approach and a more mixed media system is recommended for promotion of peace and furthering the establishment of democracies which are in the interest of the people. Production of peace, democracy, development and the socialization of journalists and audiences is discussed in the light of Africa, the Middle East, Northern Ireland, and Eastern Europe.

Source: http://globalmedia.emu.edu.tr, Global Media Journal MJ: Mediterranean Edition 2(1) Spring 2007.

The Golden Triangle: Democracy, Development and Peace

As the first decade of the 21st century comes to an end, the relationship between democracy, development and peace becomes increasingly important for the survival and well being of humanity. Without ignoring the difficulties inherent in the implementation of these links, their importance has been recognized by outstanding individuals, institutions, and movements. The decision to award the Nobel Peace Prize for 2004 to Wangari Maathai, of Kenya, stressed her contribution to sustainable development, democracy and peace. In her speech of acceptance she stated:

> . . . individuals and groups across the globe . . . work quietly and often without recognition to . . . promote democracy, defend human rights and ensure equality between women and men. By so doing, they plant seeds of peace (*www.nobelprize.org*).

A second Nobel Peace Prize laureate (1987), former President of Costa Rica and architect of the Peace Plan for Central America, Dr. Oscar Arias, delivered a similar message

> . . . of peace, democracy, and development, to the Global Peace Forum in Taipei, Taiwan in August 2001, concluding with a plea, that instead of buying destroyers, invest in development. Rather than stocking up on cruise missiles, buy schoolbooks for children . . . look outside your territory to . . . Laos and Cambodia, . . . Central America, or to those millions of Africans living in misery and helplessness (*www.nobelprize.org*).

2001 Nobel Peace laureate, former UN Secretary-General Kofi Annan, told the Third Ministerial Meeting of the Community of Democracies convening in Santiago de Chile in April 2005: Democracy and development reinforce each other, as do democracy and peace (*www.nobelprize.org*).

Social researchers and scholars have been studying the necessary conditions for a productive convergence of democracy, peace and development. In 2005, the independent, nonprofit Canadian Institute for Research on Public Policy (*www.irpp.org*) published two such studies. Democracy and Economic

Development examines the links between democracy and growth, underlines the quality of governance as an important influence on economic performance, and concludes that democratization has a positive impact on some determinants of economic development. Democracy and Peace-Building observes how democratization has become part and parcel of post-Cold War peace agreements and post-conflict peace-building efforts carried out under the auspices of the UN. In 2005, an international symposium conducted at the University of Texas, addressed the relation of sustainable development to peacemaking and peacekeeping. The point of departure was that with the end of the Cold War, the pursuit of lasting peace and an end to conflict, together with sustainable development, have become a global imperative. Accordingly, demands were made to broadly define (a) basic constitutive conditions of social life together with a social consensus over terms of peace; and (b) conceiving development as including more than providing and maintaining resource flows, to encourage communities to agree about their shared interests and to establish frameworks that facilitate social consensus and peace. The conclusion was that both peace and sustainable development could be realized only within the context of communities . . . striving to be inclusive and democratic (*www.utexas.edu/courses/sustdevt/conceptual.html*).

Communication: A Vital Feature of the Triangle

Communication has been recognized as a crucial factor in the peace-democracy-development triangle and its importance has been expressed in several approaches:

a. *The ethical-normative approach* asks "what is right and wrong in the activities of media organizations and professionals", and "what ought to be". Many brilliant thinkers[1] have developed this approach in "purist", philosophical terms. Regardless of their intellectual and critical merits, however, they have not offered applicable alternatives to the present state of affairs. They have been criticized in particular for failing to come up with viable options for linking media structures and professionals with values of democracy, peace, and development.

b. *The professional approach* is concerned with solutions to day-to-day problems and dilemmas in the activities of media organizations and professionals.

1 Such as Noam Chomsky, Edward Hermann, Robert McChesney, and Cees Hamelink.

Such problems and dilemmas can include: control, freedom of expression, responsibility, accuracy, impartiality, the public interest, personal ethics, constraints affecting journalistic coverage, development of skills such as form, technique judgment and critical thinking, depth and content, and built-in contradictions between media structures and peace-oriented/development-oriented communication (Blasi, 2004; Janeway, 2002; Hackett & Zhao, 2005; Hackett, 2006; Shinar, 2000, 2003, 2004, 2007a; Tehranian, 2002; Wolfsfeld, 2003, 2004; Zandberg & Neiger, 2005).

c. *The structural approach* considers realities of ownership and state/private interests, and their interaction with media professional standards and ethics, democratic values, socio economic development, and cultural values. Moreover, while the former approaches consider media ethics and professionalism as they relate to the individual journalist, the structural approach departs from the premises that[2]:

1. We live in a mediated environment ruled by government media monopolies or commercial media oligopolies that construct our images of the world.
2. In the present globalized/globalizing world, media ethics and professionalism must be dealt with not only individually but also in the context of media institutional, national, and international regimes.
3. Ethics (related to peace, social justice, democracy, and development) and professionalism need commensurate institutional frameworks and sanctions in order to become effective.
4. A pluralism of media content, form, and structures at the local, national, and global levels is necessary to reflect the diversity and complexity of the world.

The Communication Deficit in Democracy and Development

At the beginning of the 21st century a communication deficit can be identified in the areas of democracy and development. It is expressed in the fact that despite the growth in democratic media spaces in many parts of the world, particularly after the end of the Cold War, an increasing gap exists between mainstream official

[2] See works by Majid Tehranian, Ben Bagdikian, Robert Hackett, etc.

speak, consumer-oriented media and credible communication. A more democratic media structure including older and newer communication technologies[3] could seek to achieve a better balance between private and public social interests. This would lead to recognition of, first, the equal legitimacy of private economic considerations and of the need for public activities that do not promise immediate profit; second, the need for democratic interaction, through various media, of governments, opposition groups and other organizations, including NGOs and civil society institutions; third, the needs of the public for information and context, beyond private interests; and fourth, the need for a decrease of institutional control over communication among groups and individuals.

At present, a few transnational media corporations in the more developed countries dominate the commercial media system. Government media monopolies together with foreign economic interests control the flow of information and news in most of the less developed countries. In both authoritarian and democratic structures, domestic order and national security are claimed to determine the main ethical imperative. Commercial systems gravitate towards an ethics of freedom, i.e. rights to property and maximum profits. Public media systems have developed a notion of public service originally defined in terms of elitist cultural concepts but increasingly eroded by the competition from the commercial media (Andersen and Strate, 2000). Community media systems such as those belonging to religious or labor organizations serve their own constituencies (Howley, 2005). Finally, independent media activists, including zine-publishers and bloggers have been spreading the free blogosphere media gospel, but the digital divide and other constraints still limit its worldwide adoption at present (Don Alphonso, 2007; Sieradski, 2007; Shinar, 2007b).

A mixed media system, combining channels of all five models could provide better service. It would encourage media ethics and professional standards to activate pluralism of content and checks and balances in news coverage. This would allow for honest representation of all voices in given societies, for the development of policies and projects beneficial to their "developed", "developing", and "underdeveloped" sectors and for better representation of peace in the media.

3 The advent of the blogosphere, and the global expansion of web logs — blogs — both in number and volume, is a phenomenon that can be considered an important move in this direction, regardless of differences and gaps between continents and countries.

Conflicts and Peace in the Media: Deficit and Balance

Most post-Cold War conflicts have had a global impact, regardless of their nature as sporadic eruptions of regional violence or worldwide "democratic anti-terror crusades". Local, regional, and global interests, loyalties, and power plays have been interacting (Robertson, 1994, Sreberny-Mohammadi, 1991; Hackett, 2006), propelled by the development of communication technologies, and by increasing media usage. Some striking findings show that the media can help enhance both "peace deficits" and "peace-balanced performances". Thus:

a. The media can contribute to war, genocide, terrorism, oppression, and repression as well as to security, dignity, growth, and decision-making by citizens on the basis of accurate, credible, and manageable information (McGoldrick & Lynch 2005; Schechter, 2003).

b. The media are stakeholders of democracy together with inter-governmental organizations, global civil organizations, and transnational financial and industrial corporations (Hackett and Zhao 2005).

c. In concert with the premise that the interests of world peace and security create an urgent need to devise effective ways of handling conflict, there is need to explore mediating mechanisms that may assist in developing better understanding of conflict and better ability to reduce its impact.

d. Media structures and ethics can be adapted to the needs of democracy, peace and human development, by:

    1. Uplifting professional standards and social awareness of journalists, and their organizations;

    2. Encouraging a transition in the working logic of the media from hierarchical, hegemonic, and mobilized transmission practices to better-balanced and negotiated (with the public) transmission-reception processes;

    3. Recognizing the added value that can be contributed by newer technologies, such as web logs, to the media repertoire;

    4. Presenting honest, reliable, and autonomous representations of reality, in terms of each society and culture, rather than having them imposed by outside powers (Tehranian, 2002; Galtung, 2000; Bendaña 2004);

5. Striving to produce human and social change in individuals, groups, collectives and systems, and to develop critical awareness, and a better understanding of self and other.

The Promise of Peace Communication

Peace-oriented communication is essential for enhancing development policies as well as for encouraging the development of democratic media structures. Expectations have been growing that combinations of democratic media structures and peace communication might increase the effectiveness of development programs; reduce socio-economic inequality, corruption, and exploitation, and increase social and self-respect towards the weaker components of societies.

The promise of peace communication and its techniques, such as Peace Journalism and peace-oriented strategies of media usage[4], is based on their integrative and synthesizing roles in bridging gaps of context and linkage of information and interpretation that prevail in both the professional and the consumer end of conventional mainstream journalism. When performed effectively, they might enhance critical awareness, and encourage the change of attitudes and behavior necessary for both parties of the communication processes to recognize the value of peace-oriented and democratic media for development.

Peace journalism and peace-oriented strategies of media usage aim at improving both media representations of reality and how they are perception by the public. They propose to frame stories in broader, fairer, and more accurate terms than the ones dictated by the biases of the "ratings culture and structure", and of the interests of governments and movements. They explore and create demands for learning backgrounds and contexts of conflict formation in order to make media sources, processes, and effects more relevant.

They provide space for alternative voices and encourage an interest in learning the views of all involved parties while ensuring that conflict rather than involved parties is seen as the problem. Also they trace connections between journalists,

---

[4] For more detailed descriptions and analyses of Peace Journalism, see Conflict and Communication Online 2006, 5(2); 2007 6(1), 6(2), *www.cco.regener-online.de*; Global Media Journal: Mediterranean Edition, Fall 2006, and the current issue, *http://globalmedia.emu.edu.tr;* Lee and Maslog, 2005.

their sources, the stories they cover, and the consequences of their reporting, including the common interests of media owners and power structures. Successful outcomes of this process might introduce a better-balanced literacy and discourse of non-violence and creativity into media coverage, and enhance a different media producing and consuming consciousness. Also the adoption of these techniques can call public attention and opinion to the impact and threats of conflicts.

Performance: Does Peace-Oriented Communication Make a Difference?

Two relevant types of applications can test the performance of peace-oriented communication against their promise: the first is the introduction and use of new media structures in efforts made at conflict transformation and reconciliation. Such structures have usually followed the end of conflict in less democratic environments moving towards democracy and in less developed regions and countries. The second application is the socialization of journalists, media organizations and the public, to a different working logic. It is expressed in the production of contents and in attitudes different than those inspired by the prevailing ratings culture and structure of the media.

Media Structures

In addition to the creation of peace-oriented media structures out of a major motivation to enhance peace, many such structures have helped to strengthen democratic powers, and have become assets in development processes.

The frightening impact of "hate-media" in national wars of the 1990s, such as in Rwanda, Bosnia and Sierra Leone has produced "boomerang reactions". Rwandan Radio-Télévision Libre des Milles Collines conducted a vicious genocidal campaign inciting the slaughter of more than half a million Tutsi people in less than one hundred days. Bosnian electronic and print media also helped to promote ethnic conflict. While explicit hate messages were broadcast less frequently than in Rwanda, their cumulative impact fuelled hatred over a long period of time (Bratic, 2006).

Perhaps in reaction to this trend, an impressive number of projects have been conducted involving the implant of peace-oriented media. Bratic (2006) reports that in the last decade or so, a total of about forty media projects in 18 countries on four continents were reported as efforts at post-war conflict transformation.

In many cases they have become tools of democratization and development. In Cambodia, the success of Radio UNTAC (UN Transitional Authority) set up a model whereby subsequent UN missions (in Sierra Leone, Rwanda, Bosnia, Ethiopia, East Timor, and Kosovo), have included the operation of radio stations in their peace-building efforts. Radio UNTAC gave Cambodia, for the first time, a reliable source of nonbiased news and enabled political parties and candidates to access to the media. When the station became popular, it moved forward to perform development functions, adding music, entertainment and information programs. In East Timor, Studio Moris Hamutuk is a production facility intended to promote reconciliation between East Timor and Indonesia. Set up by Swiss-based Fondation Hirondelle, the studio provides independent and credible information, focusing exclusively on news programs, current affairs, documentaries and interviews. In Africa, the establishment of new peace-oriented media structures has been sponsored mostly by humanitarian NGOs, such as the international SFCG – Search for Common Ground, and Fondation Hirondelle, some in cooperation with UN missions.

These projects focused on the establishment of radio stations, such as UN Radio MINURCA in the Central African Republic, Sierra Leone Radio Ndeke Luka [Bird of luck] and STAR Radio in Liberia as well as on the production of peace-oriented radio contents and assistance to local journalists. Studio Ijambo, established in Burundi by SFCG in 1995, in direct response to the production and broadcasting of hate incitement and genocidal propaganda by neighboring Rwandan Radio Télévision Libre de Mille Collines (RTLM), became a model for the entire continent. Since 2002 Congolese Radio Okapi, a joint venture of Fondation Hirondelle and the UN mission, has been broadcasting from Kinshasa, capital of the Democratic Republic of Congo in local languages to almost one million refugees.

The media have played an equally significant role in European peacemaking and peace-keeping. The use of radio and television as weapons of war led to the development of new media structures in the Bosnian process of reconciliation, supported by international organizations and NGOs. The Free Exchange Radio Network (FERN) was established by OCSE (the Organization for Cooperation and Security in Europe), to provide coverage of the first post-war Bosnian elections. Later, it became a nationwide station, providing news, information and music.

Another dimension of the difference made by media organizations is the reform of previous media structures. In Bosnia, the Independent Media Commission (IMC) was established to prevent the propagation of hate messages. A similar process occurred in Kosovo, where the UN, OSCE and other international organizations helped establish a national television and radio system, and encouraged strict regulation of hate broadcasts. Like in Bosnia, in July 2000 UN media experts encouraged the system to become a public entity, thus moving from its specific peacemaking function into a fully-fledged tool for democracy and development.

Production of Peace/Democracy/Development Contents and the Socialization of Journalists and Audiences

In Africa, the establishment of peace-oriented media structures have been sponsored mostly by humanitarian NGOs, such as SFCG (in Angola, Rwanda, Burundi, and Sierra Leone), Fondation Hirondelle (in the Central African Republic, Liberia, and the Democratic Republic of Congo). In addition to the establishment of radio stations, these projects focused on the production of peace-oriented contents (news, soap operas, programs for women and children and musical shows featuring peace songs) and assistance to local journalists, such as The Hirondelle News Agency, set up to cover the Rwanda genocide trials at the International Criminal Tribunal, in Arusha, Tanzania.

Studio Ijambo in Burundi has produced peace-oriented contents that became a model for the entire continent. Under the slogan Dialogue is the future, most programs directly address the roots of the regional conflict. Three surveys conducted since 1999 indicate that 80 to 90 percent of the population listens to the local soap opera "Umubanyi Niwe Muryango" regularly.

In Latin America, the Colombian organization of journalists "Medios por la Paz" (Media for Peace) has been engaged in training and education, and in helping journalists who have been subject to violence as a result of their reporting. The organization has established archives, information networks and publications for journalists in conflict areas. One of the most prominent projects is the publication of a dictionary that lists 600 words signifying conflict or peace connotations in an attempt to "disarm language".

In the Middle East, most Israeli, Arab, and Palestinian mainstream media have not been investing serious efforts in peace-oriented communication. Some NGOs have been much more effective in this sense. Based on European sponsorship, Keshev, the Israeli Association for the Protection of Democracy, and its Palestinian counterpart Miftah, have been monitoring media coverage of the conflict, and publishing reports that have had considerable impact. In addition, Israeli-Palestinian jointly operated All for Peace Radio, has been successfully engaged in peace journalism. Common Ground News Service (a SFCG project) was established as a news agency to provide information to both sides in the conflict. The service presents coverage of the Israeli-Palestinian conflict, employs local and international experts and provides syndicated articles, analysis and op-ed pieces. Supported by the European Community and UNESCO, the service operates on a non-profit basis.

Also journalism-training organizations, such as The Institute for Further Education of Journalists (FOJO), USAID and Internews have offered courses to Palestinian journalists. SFCG has been involved in training and created an award program that recognizes journalism that contributes toward common understanding and dialogue.

Northern Ireland differs from other cases. Unlike most other conflict regions, it enjoys a fairly advanced system of commercial and public media organizations, particularly in broadcasting. Therefore, Northern Ireland has not seen the creation of new media outlets specializing in peace programming or training in peace journalism. Engaging in the socialization of its professionals and audiences, the existing Irish media structures acted as a cornerstone in support of the Stormont Castle peace negotiations and agreements.

Finally, SPEAR (Support Programming for Emergency Assistance by Radio) was a project that provided assistance to journalists from warring communities to produce peace and development oriented programs. Sponsored by Media Action International (MAI), it was originally aimed at the refugees in Macedonia, Kosovo (Serbia) and Albania. Three radio series were produced in each country. The Kosovo program *In the Name of Humanitarianism* used local broadcasters on both sides of conflict at the time when the need for humanitarian information was at its peak. Also in Macedonia, the success of "Nashe Maalo" (Our Neighborhood), a television series for children, led to its continuation as a street theatre, puppet theatre and magazine, later released as a CD soundtrack. The show was watched by 76% of the young audience regularly (SFCG, 2002).

Additional cases appear in publications such as the Berghof Handbook for Conflict Transformation (*www.berghof-handbook.net*), featuring proposals for reporting on ethno-political conflicts in a manner that fosters peace. A basic model is offered to explain the impact of media and to discuss NGO-activities and a proposal for reform efforts in Europe. A case study of the role media can play in ethno-political conflict portrays initiatives of the NGO Common Ground (in Greece, Turkey, Macedonia, Sierra Leone, and Burundi), and shares lessons concerning the design, implementation and assessment of projects aimed at cooperating with media, promoting pluralism and fostering ethical standards.

Last but not least, Loretta Hieber's *Lifeline Media* (2001) *Reaching Populations in Crisis: A Guide to Developing Media Projects in Conflict Situations*, is a guide for those involved in setting up media-related projects in conflict and post-conflict settings. Her approach is designed to ensure that affected populations always have access to well-produced humanitarian information in a manner that enhances local media capacity. Also she explores how the skills of professional Western journalists can best be applied in realizing this objective.

Problems and Dilemmas

Peace journalism and peace-oriented strategies of media usage have been exposed to professional, ethical and theoretical criticism and to practical shortcomings (Shinar 2007a). Professional, ethical and theoretical criticism is directed at the contradiction of these strategies with professional norms and with some prevailing theories of mass communication (Hanitzsch, 2004). These strategies allegedly erode journalists objectivity and integrity while making no distinction between audiences. Practical shortcomings refer to difficulties:

- Reconciling the seemingly inherent contradictions between the nature of peace stories and the professional demands of mainstream journalism.
- Producing persuasive evidence of PJ importance, news value, and feasibility, and capacity to achieve popularity and avoid rejection by mainstream journalists and audiences.
- Avoiding self-manipulation the priority given by editors (more than field reporters) to incoming items that fit their own state-of-mind, psychological pre-dispositions and news-value expectations, rather than to accept evidence from the staff in the field (Shinar and Stoiciu 1992).
- Developing a media discourse of peace, democracy, and development: Even when there is a peace process, the media are constrained by structure and culture, and by the lack of specific media discourses of peace, democracy, and development (Shinar 2004).

Strategies for Increasing the Effectiveness of Peace-Oriented, Democratic and Development-Conscious Media

Appropriate structural conditions and adequate professional socialization are essential tools, in addition to content and material resources, for enhancing the public and civic roles of the media, in the common grounds of peace, democracy, and development. Pluralism of media ownership and control is an indispensable condition for media checks and balances as well as for the production and dissemination of peace-oriented contents and forms during and after conflicts. Thus, governmental and commercial media systems could be accompanied by public and community media systems as well as by newer individual media based on state-of-the-art technologies in order to redress the balance in media structures and contents.

Moreover, media structures created or redeployed in the framework of peacemaking could be steered to also become agencies for the promotion of democracy and development when hostilities stop. Current efforts to harness the media to the promotion of peace seem to have the necessary qualities to be redressed into democratization and development efforts. In this context, it is important to regulate hate media and propaganda at all times, obviously as much as allowed by democratic procedure. Reducing the level and amount of hate messages during conflict significantly minimizes the damage the media can cause to efforts geared to peace, democracy, and development.

In a more practical vein, initiatives to facilitate peace-oriented activities offer some strategies for strengthening democratic and developmental media. Two such initiatives represent a large variety: The first is a series of activities based on the claims that:

a. Media used with professionalism and attention to preventing conflict can help to expose diverse groups to viewpoints that can make them less inclined to use violence and

b. Supporting independent media in emerging and established democracies alike helps to consolidate and nurture democracy and development: successful media projects contribute to pluralism, conflict resolution, and active, well-informed civil societies (TOOLBOX).

Such activities can include:

- Training ethnically or otherwise diverse teams of journalists to act together to present a balanced view of issues and reduce partisan reporting;
- Training reporters and editors to enhance their professional capabilities in the basics of peace-oriented communication: reporting standards, rumor control, fact-checking and validation of sources, reducing bias, the need for presenting more than one side, developing programming, teaching management techniques, attracting advertisers, and highlighting other commercial survival skills to station personnel and other media professionals;
- Conducting peace-oriented media-literacy projects for audiences, including those in educational system settings and community frameworks of different ethnic, religious, regional, and other backgrounds;
- Sponsoring conferences on media professionalization, training and sponsoring exchange visits between journalists and other media personnel;

- Engaging journalists in scriptwriting and interviewing exercises focused on avoiding stereotypes and bias in covering "the other"; developing seminars on covering "the other" in which journalists and editors can discuss problems and solutions in covering sensitive topics and in serving their diverse audience;
- Encouraging the reduction of government control of media, of media dependence on the government, of media dependence on government information, and to regulate commercial control;
- Organizing networks of independent radio/TV stations to help pool programming resources;
- Supporting equal access to the media by ethnic, religious and regional groups, with particular reference to the newer media;
- Advocating reform of peace-oriented media laws;
- Establishing and supporting indigenous institutions to monitor the media.

The second initiative suggests starting a World Media Development Bank (WMDB) as a UN specialized agency or along similar lines (Tehranian 2002). WMDB can be financed out of taxes imposed on the two communication global commons, namely the geo-stationary orbit and the electromagnetic spectrum. The privilege commercial enterprises enjoy by using a common global resource, should produce an obligation for them to contribute to a more balanced communication system. The Bank may, in turn, provide low interest loans to support independent media and interactive communication aimed at audiences with low or no media access, and committed to the above-mentioned strategies, and to peace-oriented communication ethics and practices.

Finally, while it is true that the performance of peace-oriented communication still has to stand up to its promise, given its young age, it should be given the opportunity to contribute to the peace, democracy, and development "golden triangle". It should be given the opportunity to act, try, err, and amend its performance through the use of various types of media – traditional, printed, broadcast, and online – particularly in view of the poor results achieved by other efforts.

(Dov Shinar is Professor in the School of Communication and Head of the Research Center on War and Peace Coverage at Netanya Academic College in Israel. Dr. Shinar is Principal Investigator for the Peace Journalism Group of the Toda Institute for Global Peace and Policy Research, Professor Emeritus at Concordia University, Montreal and Ben Gurion University, Israel. He can be reached at shinard@bgumail.bgu.ac.il)

References

Andersen, R. & Strate, L. (2000). Critical studies in media commercialism. Oxford: Oxford University Press.

Bendaña, A. (2004). From peace-building to state-building: One step forward and two backwards? *Transcend Bulletin*, December 2. Available from *ww.transcend.org.*

Bläsi, B. (2004). Peace journalism and the news production process. *Conflict & Communication Online*, 3. Available from: *www.cco.regener-online.de.*

Bratic, V. (2006). Examining peace-oriented media in areas of violent conflict. Paper presented at the IPRA conference, Calgary, July 1.

Don Alphonso. (2007). The big schlamassl: Blogging on the Arab-Israeli conflict from a German and German-Jewish point of view. Paper presented at the International Conference on Boundaries of Free Speech? German-Israeli Journalism behind Growing Rifts between the Western and the Muslim World, Jerusalem: Van Leer Institute, February 14-15.

Galtung, J. (2000). The task of peace journalism. *Ethical Perspectives, 7*; *http://www.ethics.be/ethics/viewpic.php?LAN=E&TABLE=EP&ID=141.*

Hackett, R. A. (2006). Is peace journalism possible? Three frameworks for assessing structure and agency in news media. *Conflict and Communication Online* 5(2). Available from: *www.cco.regener-online.de.*

Hackett, R. A. & Zhao, Y. (Eds.). (2005). *Democratizing global media: One world, many struggles.* Oxford: Rowman and Littlefield.

Hanitzsch, T. (2004). Journalists as peacekeeping force? Peace journalism and mass communication theory. *Journalism Studies*, *5*(4), 483-495.

Hieber, L. (2001). Lifeline media: Reaching populations in crisis. A guide to developing media projects in conflict situations. Geneva: Media Action International (MAI).

Howley, C. (2005). Community media: People, places, and communication technologies. UK: Cambridge University Press.

Janeway, M. (2002) Rethinking the lessons of journalism school, *The New York Times*. 17 August: A11, URL *http://www.nytimes.com/2002/08/17/opinion/17JANE.html?todaysheadlines*

Lee, S. T. & Maslog, C. C. (2005). War or peace journalism? Asian newspaper coverage of conflicts. *Journal of Communication, 5*(2), 311-329.

McGoldrick, A. & Lynch, J. (2005). *Peace journalism*. UK: Hawthorn Press.

Robertson, R. (1994). Globalisation or glocalisation? *The Journal of International Communication. 1*(1), 33-52.

Schechter, D. (2003). *Embedded: Weapons of mass deception*. Amherst, NY: Prometheus.

Shinar, D. (2000). Media diplomacy and peace talk : The Middle East and Northern Ireland. *Gazette, 62*(2) April, 83-98.

Shinar, D. (2003). Peace process in cultural conflict: The role of the media. *Conflict and Communication Online*: Special Issue. Available from *www.cco.regener-online.de*.

Shinar, D. (2004). Media peace discourse: Constraints, concepts and building blocks. *Conflict and Communication Online. 3*(1-2). Available from *www.cco.regener-online.de*

Shinar, D. (2007a). Epilogue peace journalism: The state of the art. *Conflict and Communication Online. 6*(1), forthcoming. Available from: *www.cco.regener-online.de*

Shinar, D. (2007b). Differences of boundaries of free speech in different media. Paper presented at the International Conference on Boundaries of Free Speech? German-Israeli Journalism behind Growing Rifts between the Western and the Muslim World. Jerusalem: Van Leer Institute, February 14-15.

Shinar, D. & Stoiciu, G. (1992). Media representations of socio-political conflict: The Romanian Revolution and the Gulf War, *Gazette, 50*, 243-257.

Sieradski, D. (2007) The spin cycle: How bloggers and columnists are shaping our perception of world events. Paper presented at the International Conference on Boundaries of Free Speech? German-Israeli Journalism behind Growing Rifts between the Western and the Muslim World, Jerusalem: Van Leer Institute, February 14-15.

Sreberny-Mohammadi, A. (1991). The global and the local in international communications. In J. Curran & M. Gurevitch (Eds.), *Mass media and society* (pp. 118-138). London: Edward Arnold.

Tehranian, M. (2002). Peace journalism: Negotiating global media ethics. *Harvard Journal of Press/Politics, 7*(2), April, 58-83.

Toolbox: *http://www.caii.com/CAIIStaff/Dashboard_GIROAdminCAIIStaff/Dashboard_CAIIAdminDatabase/resourc es/ghai/toolbox.htm.*

www.utexas.edu/courses/sustdevt/conceptual.html

Wolfsfeld, G. (2004). *Media and the path to peace*. UK: Cambridge University Press.

www.berghof-handbook.net, http://www.berghof-handbook.net/articles/reljic_handbook.pdf; http://www.berghof-handbook.net/articles/melone_hb.pdf

Zandberg, E. & Neiger, M. (2005). Between the nation and the profession: Journalists as members of contradicting communities. *Media, Culture & Society*, *27*(1), 131-141.

4

Structural and Social Forces Restricting Media News Content in Democracies

A Critical Perspective

Gregg A Payne

This essay offers a critical perspective of the news product generated by US media. It is argued that social and structural conditions dictating content are similar to those affecting media artifacts of authoritarian political regimes. Media are seen under both political conditions to be tools of elite interests preoccupied with ideological control of social, political, and economic environments. The contention is that in both democratic and authoritarian political circumstances, the news product is homogenized, offering little by way of divergent perspectives. The consequent information deprivation is linked to an impoverished public discourse that is antithetical to democratic process.

Source: www.scientificjournals.org. This article was originally published in the Journal of Humanities and Social Sciences, Volume 2, Issue 1, 2008 published by Scientific Journals International.

Introduction

This essay argues that a concatenated set of structural and social forces contribute to homogenization of mass media news content, and that the homogenization naturalizes a distorted reality by foregrounding myths and narratives serving elite interests. As the term is used here, content homogenization suggests that events and topics selected for news coverage and the ideological perspectives with which they are infused, provide little in the way of diversity, contribute little to a free marketplace of ideas (Gitlin, 2003, p. 211, 271), and, as a consequence, subvert democratic process. The consequence of homogenization is an impoverished ideological diversity favoring elites and significantly abridging interpretations of reality that can be reasonably assigned and debated by media content consumers (Slater, 2007; Mapes, 2005; Gitlin, 2003, p. 6; Lee and Solomon, 1991; Herman and Chomsky, 1988; Postman, 1985; Schudson, 1972, pp. 160-194).

The concern here is with exposing forces producing content homogenization, their provenance in market economies, and the resulting inherent tension with democratic institutions. The contention is that the homogenizing forces are similar in hegemonic effect to those operating upon media artifacts of authoritarian political regimes (McChesney, 2002). They reflect the priorities of the relative few who dominate news production operations, including the very rich, chief executives, the corporate rich, senior members of the military, and the political directorate, all representing a relatively monolithic presence in their acceptance of a common set of values, beliefs, attitudes, perspectives, norms, rules, and behaviors (Mills, 1956; Gans, 1980, p. 206-213). These are the same castes that comprise a media elite constituted of ownership and senior executives, whose usually unobtrusive machinations as superordinate gatekeepers dictate media content (Schudson, 2005; Gitlin 2003). This helps explain why media in the US are principally business enterprises, why many are increasingly skewed to the political right (Hallin, and Mancini, 2005; Sheen, 2002), why, because of high entry costs, they tend to be the exclusive province of the rich and powerful (Curran, 2005), and why content decisions are the product of profit imperatives.

Beyond gatekeeping, and its influence over both media and public agendas, central homogenizing influences include media consolidation, information subsidies, news sourcing, pack journalism, wire services and syndicates, and advertising.

Agenda Setting

The media agenda (McCombs and Shaw, 1972) is the product of shared ideological commitments of economic elites, including media ownership, and dominate political and social forces, whose influence limits reportorial possibilities. Where, as a consequence, the media agenda emerges as a homogenized news product, it becomes the public agenda, reflecting a hegemonic confluence of external and internal interests typified by the conservative positions of those occupying senior status in the gatekeeping hierarchy, and subscribed to as a matter of both organizational efficacy and self preservation by those functioning in subordinate gatekeeping roles (Tunstall, 2008, pp. 110-111; Gans, 2003, p. 34; Gitlin, 2003; Tuchman, 1978, p. 5). The resulting insular and parochial news product is characterized by a mendacious topical, thematic, and ideological sterility, imposing on consumers a restricted set of perceptual and cognitive filters. The consequent information deprivation produces conditions in which media-influenced social control can be linked to pluralistic ignorance, a spiral of silence, and a desiccated public discourse (Noelle-Neumann, 1984, 1991; Gans, 1980, p. 294).

Any apparent ideological disjunctions in the news product are readily resolved within the context of the larger commitment of gatekeepers to narratives that maintain social, economic, and political stability (Gans, 2003, p. 11; Infante, Rancer, and Womak, 1990, pp. 31, 346, 349-350). Distinctions drawn between conservative and liberal economic policy and democracy as it is practiced in the US rarely, if ever, exceed the confines of a dogmatic dedication to the orthodoxy of capitalist economic systems and democracy American style (Lewis, Chomsky, and Herman, 1997). It is hardly surprising that news is characterized by a pro-business bias (Gans, 2003, p.63-67). Infected by devotion to a conventional wisdom that declines to recognize viewpoints reaching beyond what everyone is assumed to know or believe (Mapes, 2005, p. 273), news serves multiple fundamental functions. It works to justify an existing social structure characterized by inequitable distribution of life chances, extols the probity of the elite, and, where transgressions are too egregious to ignore, offers exculpatory rationalizations.

Media Consolidation

Further ensuring homogenization of news content, profit expectations of ownership, including shareholders, have provided the impetus for media consolidation (Gans, 2003, pp. 22-28; McChesney, 2002, p. 15, 20; Powell, W. 1987, pp. 53-63). Economic influences have resulted in 97 percent of US daily newspapers operating as local monopolies, with almost half owned by a group or chain (Jamieson and Campbell, 2006, p. 169). The trend, perhaps, began with the ascension of the *New York Times* in 1967 to de facto monopoly status (Tunstall, 2008, p. 109), and has accelerated since (Bertrand, 2003). Among the consequences of consolidation is a restrictive influence on the number and diversity of permissible news subjects. News organizations routinely use media channels to press corporate agendas consistent with a probusiness, market economy ideology, diminishing the plurality of perspectives available to the public (Jamieson and Campbell, 2006, pp. 166, 168.169; Gans, 2003, p. 8, 26). Between 1981 and 2000, the number of organizations controlling most of the daily newspaper, motion picture, television, magazine, and book production in the United States shrunk by 50 percent, from 46 to 23 corporations (Bagdikian, 2000).

In addition to ownership, interlocking directorates exert influence over the news product. Members of boards of directors in various industries having substantial political, social, and economic influence, including control over advertising dollars, the sine qua non of media commercial success, can also be found as consorts populating media boards of directors (Sheen, 2002; Lewis, J., Chomsky, N., and Herman E., 1997; Gandy, 1982, p. 201). Effectively, mass communication in the US is an oligopoly controlled by an oligarchy, with corporations having gained monopolistic control over the mass media product (Chomsky, 2002).

Information Subsidies

The incestuous relationship involving interlocking directorates is reinforced through information subsidies, particularly news releases, generated as public relations products on behalf of government, business, the military, and other superordinate institutions. The fundamental responsibility of public relations practitioners, operating as surrogates for senior gatekeepers, is to make institutions represented look good, using media as conduits to link clienteles with the public. Both because it is free and because it is ideologically consonant with priorities of employers, the ersatz news so produced and made available to mass media enterprises for use at no cost is eagerly embraced by the gatekeeping establishment. As a homogenizing influence, it represents conservatively 60 percent of all mediated news material (Gandy, p. 12). The ubiquity of the product is illustrated further by the number of public relations workers engaged in the image-making, maintenance and repair business. It is estimated that there are some 150,000 in the US alone, and as many as 1.5 million globally (Cutlip, Center, and Broom, 2003). By one estimate, some 13,000 work for the US government, spending annually something on the order of $2.5 billion in their campaign to convince the public, using media channels, that what the government does is both good and well done (Lee, M., and Solomon, N., 1992).

Institutional Spokespersons

Conceptually, public relations is multi-dimensional, operating in a number of guises. Institutional spokespersons fulfill a public relations role, crafting messages that contribute to a pallid, homogenized news product consistent with the need of senior gatekeepers to control the media agenda.

Journalistic convention mandates the appearance of objectivity. The appearance is secured through use, generally unleavened by responsible journalistic skepticism, of quotes or similar sorts of attribution originating with sources who are represented as unbiased experts or disinterested observers (Tunstall, 2008, p. 117; Gitlin, 2003, p. 37; Aufderheide, 2002, p. 13; McChesney, 2002, p. 18). In fact, sources may be more accurately viewed as filters, typically front men – or women – for an institutional entity with a vested interest in ensuring an ideological spin acceptable to those in power (Curran, 2005; Tuchman, 1978, pp. 94-95). Engaging in de facto censorship, these institutionally-anointed spokespersons are assigned the function of controlling the organizational message. They are typically the sole point of contact between media representatives, who tend to adopt the institutional world view dispensed on behalf of the powerful (Tunstall, 2008, 119; Gitlin, 2003, p. 263), and to reproduce for public consumption whatever hopeful, unambiguous rendition of reality the institution is intent upon selling (Schudson,

2005; Gitlin, 2003; Lee and Solomon, 1991; Gans, 1980, pp. 116-145). This difficulty is compounded by several factors. Deadlines often militate against journalistic enterprise in seeking out alternative sources (Gans, 1980, p. 116). So do related costs, indolence, and indifference (Gitlin, 2003, 35; Tunstall, 2008, p. 107). There are expectations that divergent views – and those who expose them – will likely be exorcised, in the first case, from reportage, and, in the second, from the fraternity.

Pack Journalism

To avoid that fate, reporters and low-level editors laboring in subordinate gatekeeping roles, engage in a discourse in which news is consensually defined (Bertrand, 2003, p. 8; Gans, 1980, p. 83; Tuchman, 1978, p. 35, 59, 78). The process and consequences are akin to what Shaw has labeled consensus journalism (Biagi, 2007, p. 246), and what Crouse (1972) has called pack journalism. What is newsworthy and why, as well as the interpretation to be imposed, is a matter of collective determination that produces a largely undifferentiated product, contextualized within the ideological and normative constraints imposed by owners and managers and learned by journalists (Schudson, 2005; Gitlin, 2003, pp. 98-99). The consensual definition of news precludes the need for exercise of costly initiative in seeking out alternative perspectives. Moreover, some sufficiently revered newspapers, notably the *New York Times*, are institutional contributors to the pack mentality, suggesting through their coverage the paths to be followed by others (Gitlin, 2003, p. 299, 301). There is thus ensured content conformance with express and implied edicts of ownership and management, with subordinate levels of gatekeepers functioning as intermediaries between the dominate few at the apex of the news production pyramid and the ultimate recipients of the product, the citizen public (Baran, S., and Davis, D., 2003).

Wire Services and Syndicates

Wire services and syndicates contribute also to homogenization (Rantanen and Boyd-Barrett, 2004, p. 35; Gitlin, 2003, pp. 2-3). As a notable example, the Associated Press wields monopolistic influence in the US, and has an extensive international presence (Tunstall, 2008, 116). The AP distributes 24 hours a day, seven days a week, the same content to 1,700 US daily, weekly, and college newspapers; 5,000 radio and television outlets, 1,000 radio network affiliates, 330 international broadcasters, and 8,500 international subscribers in 121 countries, and does so in five languages: English, German, Dutch, French, and Spanish (Associated Press, 2006). Circumstances are similar with Reuters, which bills itself as "among the most read news sources. . . .reaching millions," (Reuters, 2006), and other similar operations *(hao://about.reuters.com/invcstors/ comin; 612012006)*. Subscription to such services is driven by profit imperatives. It is cheaper for media outlets to thus secure news than it is for them to individually staff bureaus around the globe. The same applies to syndicates, which also sell material for simultaneous dissemination by multiple media outlets (Biagi, 2005, p. 62).

Advertising

Advertising is another significant homogenizing influence. Notable among advertiser requirements is a hospitable news context congruent with elite constructions of reality, and directed to large, predictably sympathetic demographic categories (Schudson, 2005; Sheen, 2002; Gans, 2003, p. 21, 44; Tunstall, 1987; Gitlin, 1980, p. 216). The targeted categories turn out to be middle, upper middle, and upper classes, whose buying power and interests are relatively certain, and whose values, attitudes, and beliefs are, for the most part, ideologically consonant with those of the socially, politically, and economically dominate (Curran, 2005; Gandy, 1982, pp. 178-187; Gans, 1980, p. 61). That congruence is directly reflected in the failure of homogenized media news presentations to offer alternative possible interpretations of what are cast as unambiguous realities, unassailable norms, and settled social rules. The congruence entertains no substantive alternatives to the status quo. There is a virtual total absence of any meaningful discussion of circumstances, problems, and possible solutions associated with needs of marginal populations lacking the economic and political wherewithal to participate effectively in the conduct of democracy or free enterprise institutions (Schiller, 1996). The bias produces a knowledge gap effectively precluding the marginalized, and any who might serve as their surrogates, from engagement in substantive public discourse (Tunstall, 2008, pp. 106-107).

Consequences

The consequences of the relationships sketched here are foundational to a propaganda model of mass media content and intent. Among media functions is the integration of individuals into societies through inculcation of values, beliefs, attitudes, and behaviors consistent with those espoused by elites. The goal is achievable in the economic and political economies of the US only through concerted, propagandistic mass media manipulation consistent with practices of totalitarian regimes, in which news production conventions serve political interests (Paul and Elder, 2006, p. 8, 19; Curran, 2005; McChesney, 2002, p. 17; Chomsky, 2002; Herman and Chomsky, 1988, p. 1; Tuchman, 1978, p.83).

The argument advanced by this essay is that the structural and derivative social relationships illustrated produce a news product that is conservative (Gans, 2003, p. 47; Lewis, Chomsky and Herman, 1997), and homogenized, depicting in choice and treatment of events cast as news the ideological commitments of a controlling elite whose continued political and social prosperity is predicated upon economic dominance, and is contingent upon maintaining the status quo (Curran, 2005). The objectives and the consequences of news produced under such conditions are obfuscatory. While preferred meanings imposed by mass media are occasionally contested in the public sphere, it is generally conceded that the contest is waged between grossly unequal opponents, and any shifts in a socially constructed reality evanescent (Gamson, Croteau, Hoynes, and Sasson, 1992; Ryan, 1991; Hallin, 1987). Potential alternative realities, in particular those reflecting liberal perspectives, are left unilluminated. They are absent from what and how publics think, the things they talk about, (Curran, 2005), and, consequently, cannot influence public behavior. What emerges is a narrowly circumscribed public agenda and discourse that is antithetical to democratic process.

Media content that distorts, obscures, or fails to articulate divergent perspectives and possibilities retards public discourse, and feeds the kind of nihilism that contributes substantially to a social pathology defined symptomatically by apathy and isolation (Gamson, Croteau, Hoynes, and Sassoon, 1992; Putnam, 2001). It may also contribute ultimately to the unraveling of communal instincts, the degradation of social cohesion, and reactionary, sometimes violent, social protest.

(Gregg A Payne, Ph.D., Assistant Professor, Chapman University. The author can be reached at gpayne@chapman.edu).

References

Aufderheide, P. (2002). All-to-reality TV: Challenges for television journalists after September 11. *Journalism* 3(1), 7-36.

Bagdikian, B. (2000). *The media monopoly.* (6th ed). Beacon Press: Boston.

Baran, S., and Davis, D. (2003). *Mass communication theory: Foundations, ferment and future.* (7th ed.). Belmont, CA: Thomson/Wadsworth.

Bertrand, J. (Ed.). (2003). *An arsenal for democracy: Media accountability systems.* Hampton Press: Cresskill, NJ.

Biagi, S. (2007). Media/Impact: An introduction to mass media. (8th ed). Thomson Wadsworth: Belmont, CA.

Chomsky, N. (2002). *Media control: The spectacular achievements of propaganda.* (2nd ed.). New York: Seven Stories Press.

Crouse, T. (1972). *The boys on the bus: Riding with the campaign press corps.* New York: Random House.

Curran, J. (2005). Mediations of democracy. In J. Curran, & M. Gurevitch (Eds.), *Mass media and society* (pp. 122-152). London: Hodder Arnold.

Cutlip, S., Center, A, and Broom, G. (2003). *Effective public relations.* (91h ed.). Upper Saddle River, NJ: Prentice Hall.

Gamson, W., Croteau, D., Hoynes, W., and Sasson, T. (1992). *Media images and the social construction of reality.* Annual Review of Sociology (93), 373-393.

Gandy, O. (1982). *Beyond agenda setting: Information subsidies and public policy.* Norwood, NJ: Ablex.

Gans, H. (1980). *Deciding what's news: A study of CBS Evening News, NBC Nightly News, Newsweek, and Time.* New York: Vintage Books.

Gans, H. (2003). *Democracy and the news.* Oxford: Oxford University Press.

Gitlin, T. (2003). *The whole world is watching: Mass media in making and unmaking of the new left.* Berkley: University of California Press.

Hallin, D. (1987). Hegemony: The American news media from Vietnam to El Salvador. In D. Paletz (Ed.), *Political communication research* (pp. 3-25). Norwood, NJ: Ablex.

Hallin, D., and Mancini, P., Schudson, M. (2005). Four approaches to the sociology of news. In J. Curran, & M. Gurevitch (Eds.), *Mass media and society* (pp. 215- 233). London: Hodder Arnold.

Herman, E., and Chomsky, N. (1988). *Manufacturing consent: The political economy of the mass media.* New York: Pantheon.

Infante, D., Rancer, A,, and Womak, D. (1990). *Building communication theory.* Prospect Heights, IL: Waveland Press.

Jamieson, K, and Campbell, K. (2006). *The interplay of influence: News, advertising, politics and the Internet.* Belmont, CA: Wadsworth.

Lee, M., and Solomon, N. (1991). *Unreliable sources: A guide to detecting bias in news media.* New York: Carol Publishing.

Mapes, M. (2005). *Truth and duty: The press, the President, and the privilege of power.* New York: St. Martins Press.

McChesney, R. (2002). The US news media and world war III. *Journalism* (3)1, 14-21.

McCombs, M., and Shaw, D. (1972). The agenda setting function of mass media. *Public Opinion Quarterly*, 36, 176-187.

Media Education Foundation (Producer). (1997). Lewis, J., Chomsky, N., and Herman E. Presenters. *The myth of the liberal media.* [Motion picture]. (Available from Media Education Foundation, Northhampton, MA.).

Mills, C. (1956). *The power elite.* New York: Oxford University Press.

Noelle-Neumann, E. (1 984). *The Spiral of Silence: Public Opinion—Our social skin.* Chicago: University of Chicago.

Noelle-Neumann, E. (1991). *The theory of public opinion: The concept of the Spiral of Silence. In* 3. *A.* Anderson (Ed.), Communication Yearbook, 14, 256-287. Newbury Park, CA: Sage.

O Brien, T. (2005, February 13). Spinning frenzy: P.R.'s bad press. *The New York Times*, Section 3, p. 1.

Off the Couch Films (Producer). (2002). Sheen, M., Presenter. Project censored: Is the press really free? [Motion Picture]. (Available from California State University, Sonoma: Sonoma, CA.)

Paul, R., and Elder, L. (2006). *How to detect media bias and propaganda.* Foundation for Critical Thinking: Tomles, CA.

Postman, N. (1985). *Amusing ourselves to death: Public discourse in the age of show business.* New York: Penguin Books.

Powell, W. (1987). The blockbuster decades: The media as big business. In D. Lazere (Ed.) American media and mass culture: Left perspectives (pp. 52-63). Berkeley, CA.: University of California Press.

Putnam, R. (2001). Bowling alone: The collapse and revival of American community. New York: Touchstone.

Rantanen, T., and Oliver, B. (2004). Global and national news agencies: The unstable nexus. In A. deBeer, & Merrill, J. (Eds.), *Global journalism: Topical issues and media systems.* Boston: Pearson.

Ryan, C. (1991). *Prime Time Activism.* Boston: South End Press.

Schiller, H. (1996). *Information inequality: The deepening social crisis in America.* New York: Routledge.

Schudson, M. (2005). Four approaches to the sociology of news. In J. Curran, & M. Gurevitch (Eds.), *Mass media and society* (pp. 198-214). London: Hodder Arnold.

Schudson, M. (1972). Discovering the news: A social history of American newspapers. New York: Basic Books.

Slater, M. (2007). Reinforcing spirals: The mutual influence of media selectivity and media effects and their impact on individual behavior and social identity. *Communication Theory* 17(3), 281-303.

Tuchman, G. (1978). *Making news: A study in the construction of reality.* London: The

Free Press.

Tunstall, J. (1987). Stars, Status, Mobility. In D. Lazere (Ed.), *American media and mass culture: A left perspective* (pp. 116-123). Berkeley, CA.: University of California Press.

Tunstall, J. (2008). *The media were American: US mass media in decline.* New York: Oxford University Press.

Associated Press (2006). *About AP.* Retrieved October 20, 2006, from *http://ap.org/pages/about/about.html.*2;0 12006.

Reuters (2006). *About Reuters.* Retrieved October 20, 2006, from *http://about.reuters.com/home/.6;*1 20 12006.

5

BOOK REVIEW

Media in New Democracies

Agents for Change or Beneficiaries of Change?

Sallie Hughes

This article is a review of the book "Negotiating Democracy: Media Transformations in Emerging Democracies", edited by Isaac A Blankson and Patrick D Murphy, the main strength of which is that it covers countries that do not normally get included. It assesses the relationship between media and democracy within the broader framework of globalization regarding economic liberalism. It informs about various individual media systems in new and emerging democracies and how they contend with transitions from authoritarian rule in a global environment favoring economic liberalization. With the terms of reference established on geopolitical history of media and globalization, it also looks at electoral democracy on media ownership and content, and media interaction with discourses on democratic rights and practices.

Source: http://www.tfd.org.tw/english/tjd © Taiwan Foundation for Democracy. Reprinted with permission. This article was first published in Taiwan Journal of Democracy, Vol. 4, No. 1:187-191, July 2008.

A number of volumes comparing political, economic, and social trajectories of national media systems have appeared in recent years, but few look specifically at the experiences of new democracies and none that I can think of include such a wide variety of countries as *Negotiating Democracy: Media Transformations in Emerging Democracies*, edited by Isaac A Blankson and Patrick D Murphy. The inclusion of countries that less frequently reach the US-based academic press is the strength of this volume. The quality of several of the case studies also makes the book worth reading. Essentially a compendium of descriptive chapters on a large number of country cases less known to the field, *Negotiating Democracy* does not present a cohesive comparative framework for theory building. Therefore, this volume can be read with Curran and Park's *De-Westernizing Media Studies*, Morris and Waisbord's *Media and Globalization*, and a few others. Hanitsch's developing project, *Worlds of Journalism*, also is promising, as he and a team of researchers around the globe assess journalistic culture along a series of theoretically derived dimensions.

The purpose of *Negotiating Democracy* is to assess the relationship between media and democracy within the broader framework of globalization, especially the effects of the spread of economic liberalism and electoral democracy on media ownership and content, as well as the interaction between media and discourses on democratic rights and practices. As Murphy states, *Negotiating Democracy* "takes as its focus the place of mass media in the political and cultural life of nations negotiating democratization while simultaneously contending with economic liberalization and privatization, the changing state, and the reformation of civil society" (p. 2).

The book begins with a brief introduction from Murphy that reviews the geopolitical history of media and globalization, making the important point that neoliberalism seems to link international and intranational actors more seamlessly than political and economic flows under colonialism or during the Cold War. Liberalization of media systems, he further notes, has largely been pursued to create business opportunities and lighten the load of overburdened states, not to deepen citizenship or improve the quality of democratic practice. Quoting a 2006 observation of Peruvian scholar Rosa Maria Alfaro, he asserts this is troubling because the contours of democracy are packaged in terms of consumerism instead of citizenship.

The introduction covers much ground and makes interesting points. It should be more tightly connected to the chapters that follow, though. For example, the "hope" created by "citizen-based" media that is mentioned in the introduction might have led into a discussion of Rampal and Wilkinson's interpretations of the importance of the civic-oriented independent media early in Taiwanese and Mexican political liberalization processes. Likewise, McDaniel's discussion of NGO-based media production in Cambodia as a foil to media controlled by political patronage, or Krady's fascinating analysis of how pan-Arab audience interpretations of reality television have created a discursive space for democratic contestation, could have been explored.

The book is organized in three sections, without an integrating conclusion, introductory overviews, or guiding logic. The chapters can be understood separately and all individually offer interesting lessons for scholars and upper-level undergraduates or graduate students.

The first set of chapters covers regional trends by reviewing the challenges of media independence and pluralism in Africa, the monopolistic and quasi-monopolistic family-owned broadcast companies of Central America, and differences in the levels of media development, effects of European communications policy, and roles of media in ethnic conflict in Eastern European countries. The second section discusses state control and democratic reform in Cambodia, Taiwan, Nigeria, Iran, and South Korea. The third set of chapters assesses broadcasting and globalization in the Middle East, Mexico, Bulgaria, and Greece.

The most sophisticated chapter, in my opinion, is Kraidy's assessment of reality television and politics in the Arab world. By comparing public discourse surrounding three popular reality shows beamed on pan-Arab satellite television, he explains how business and religious leaders in several Arab countries created an arena for debate about the role of mass media and politically relevant cultural values. Further, a discussion of the potential and limitations of audience "participation" in the selection of winning program contestants illuminates how entertainment programming may influence democratic values and practices. In all, the chapter paints a picture of an emerging public sphere in which groups driven by economic, nationalistic, and religious motivations vie for control of media entertainment programming that engages audiences whose members are becoming more participatory but have yet to become fully invested democratic citizens.

Most of the remaining chapters use historical narrative to introduce readers to the media systems and contemporary issues they review. Several have interesting stories to tell. Rockwell describes media oligarchs' capture of state regulatory power in Central America. Ibroscheva and Raicheva-Stover describe how Rupert Murdoch came to control Bulgaria's strongest national network, and flooded it with translations from his US-based Fox network. Semati explores the ebbs and flows of Iranian reformers' struggles to pluralize news and public debate, but unfortunately was not able to assess trends under the current Ahmadinejad government by the time the book went to press. Sims argues that a convergence of business and political interests drove Greek radio privatization, creating a quid pro quo reminiscent of Mexican and Central American broadcasting. Other chapters provide useful overviews of media system development during democratic transitions, although they sometimes lack depth of analysis.

It is interesting to note that several of the chapters (Cambodia, Nigeria, pan-Africa, and South Korea) may not be sufficiently critical in their view of the democratizing potential of economic liberalism for mass media reform, even though other chapters (Greece, Bulgaria, Central America) are quite explicit in their descriptions of the shortcomings of faith in the market. Latin Americanists are aware that authoritarianism and private-sector media can co-exist for substantial periods of time and that structures created during authoritarian periods continue to shape media-state relations in more democratic periods. Likewise, critical political economists in established democracies have long argued that commercial media systems also support the status quo power structures in an electorally democratic society, including dominant ideologies and the actors benefiting from them. Both groups of scholars understand that media commercialism is as much a guarantee for sensationalism and depolitization of journalistic content as it is for the creation of journalistic cultures and structures holding power accountable or promoting political and ideological pluralism. Given also what seems to be a pattern of hypercommercialization of broadcast media and loss of identity in the oppositional press following founding democratic elections in many new democracies, the editors could have brought up this point during revision or in an integrating conclusion to the book.

Another debatable point is that the case selection for the book is justified only in that the countries are all undergoing political transition from different forms of authoritarianism while simultaneously under pressure to liberalize their economies. It would have been instructive to have selected cases based upon key analytical variables, if not to have explored a typology of new democracies. Some lines of analysis that might have been fruitful include the different starting points and pathways of transitions and their effects on, or interaction with, media system development; how globalization differentially affects national media systems in relation to countries' ability to produce and export media content; and how national media policies before and after the installation of democratic elections speeds or slows content commercialization and the strength of citizen-focused media.

Path dependencies and holdover authoritarian structures and cultural understandings mean that the starting point matters for media transitions. Eastern European countries are transiting from totalitarian regimes and, from what I understand, most hope to completely erase vestiges of the old state-controlled systems. Guatemala, El Salvador, and Nicaragua still face problems associated with their civil wars, and the media systems that supported the most conservative elements of those wars continue without substantial modification in the first two countries. Africa is moving away from personalistic military dictatorships, but unevenly and with fears of reversal in some countries.

Of the cases in the volume, Mexico, Taiwan, South Korea, Greece, Lebanon, and Bahrain are strong enough economically to be regional media exporters, and government policy in all but the last case seems to have supported the growth of private media either directly or, in the case of Greece, indirectly. The rest (Guatemala, El Salvador, Nicaragua, Panama, Honduras, Costa Rica, Cambodia, Romania, Bulgaria, Iran, Nigeria, Ghana, Mali, Kenya, and other emerging African democracies) have weaker domestic production capacities, varying by levels of economic development and the nature of media policy content and stability. What can we learn about media system transitions, globalization, and democracy by comparing these experiences among types of countries? This would have been an interesting question to explore.

As for journalism and the public sphere, to a greater or lesser extent, the Mexican, Taiwanese, and Greek media systems moved from authoritarianism though more civic-oriented periods, during which a section of the independent media engaged prodemocracy forces, and eventually created hybrid regimes in which the market and political connections drive broadcast news production and the weakened independent press follows mixed commercial, professional, and political logics. Are there lessons here for Nigeria, Cambodia, or other states still consolidating democratic elections and, as importantly, for the rule of law? Can the comparison tell us how Taiwan, Mexico, Greece, and other neoliberal democracies might yet create media systems that deepen democratic accountability and political pluralism?

Another theme running through several chapters is how restrictive press environments in new democracies create conditions for self-censorship and restrict diversity in media sources and content. The threat of violence, holdover authoritarian press laws, and the fear of political system reversals that are faced by African journalists similarly threaten the development of autonomous journalism in Central American and many other new democracies.

The force of transnational media conglomerates is another comparative dimension worth exploring. While foreign capital came to control Bulgaria's premier private TV network as an outlet for content created elsewhere, in South Korea, second-tier domestic commercial groups partnered with international finance and media companies to produce formidable regional media players. With the exception of Guatemala, Central America's media families have blocked such incursions. Mexico's two national broadcast networks have ties to US media conglomerates, most recently NBC, which is owned by General Electric. These transnational linkages are strengthening, even as the Mexican state finds itself unable or unwilling to open up the broadcasting spectrum to further commercial competitors or to noncommercial projects.

Considering the current US administration's portrayal of Iran as a nuclear threat, I would certainly like to better understand the potential of democratic reformers and independent media in the country. Comparative analysis could help test assumptions about both groups. While Iran's unique state structure institutionalizes religion in governance, the struggle between religious conservatives and liberalizing reformers to control the media and over whether to open them to greater pluralism and democratic debate as described in Semati's chapter evokes struggles between conservatives and reformers in other societies in which liberal democracy is not, or was not, an assured conclusion. Not to discount the differences in religious and military actors, the tango between military censors and democratic reformers using cultural magazines and other independent publications to further democratization as South American military government decompressed could share similarities with the Iranian situation as well as highlight instructive differences.

In short, *Negotiating Democracy* offers to students a number of interesting descriptions of individual media systems in new or emerging democracies as they contend with transitions from authoritarian rule in a global environment favoring economic liberalization. It does not offer an overall framework for the study of media systems in transition or propose a set of analytical dimensions for researchers to use in comparative research. However, the book raises provocative questions for those interested in media and democracy and offers raw material for scholars to use in designing future studies.

(Sallie Hughes is a PhD, Associate Professor, Journalism Program, School of Communication, University of Miami. The author can be reached at shughes@ miami.edu).

6

Democracy in the Media Society

Changing Media Structures – Changing Political Communication?

Jens Lucht and Linards Udris

This paper examines how more and more attempts are being made to draw readers away from traditional newspapers and increasing legal and financial pressures on public service broadcasting lowers the quality of programming. Even more mergers of big media organizations with capital (and media power) are becoming concentrated in fewer hands, with growing importance of 'free dailies' distributed in big European cities which tabloidize news structures and deconstruct them homogeneously. The essential findings show that in Western style democracies, the press has disentangled itself from their former social and political ties to a mode of increasing commercialization leading to a diffusion of 'media logics' into political communication and its further media dissemination as a whole.

Ever more mergers of big media organizations with capital (and media power) becoming concentrated in fewer hands, growing importance of boulevard-like "free dailies" distributed in big European cities that seem to draw readers away from traditional newspapers, and increasing legal and financial pressures on public service broadcasting that lowers the quality of programming – the structures of the media are changing considerably. These problem diagnoses can be heard in several European countries. However, complaints about changing media structures are old, and media structures still are quite different when we look at a large number of European countries. Furthermore, if media structures are changing: does this mean the content of the media and political communication itself is changing as well? If we see growing media concentration and tabloidization on the level of structures, do we then see more scandals, more infotainment and more drama in political reporting on the level of media content?

All in all, to evaluate changes of media structures, we need an empirical comparative basis, both in a diachronic (over time) and cross-country perspective. And we need a research design that connects the structural aspect of the media with the content side of the media.

In a project funded by the SNF (NCCR Challenges to Democracy in the 21st Century), we analyze the transformation of media structures and possible effects on public communication. Which structural changes have affected the media since the last third of the 20th century, and which effects do they have on political communication?

Approach

We argue for a research design that connects the structural and content side of the media, presenting indicators and their operationalization to measure the transformation of media structures across countries and over time and to link them to indicators of changing political communication (content analyses). To build a basis for the evaluation of trends and situations in the various media systems of the "three models of media and politics" (i.e. polarized plural, democratic corporatist, liberal) elaborated in Hallin/Mancini (2004), we systematically analyze and compare the cases of France (polarized pluralist), Austria, Germany, Switzerland (all democratic-corporatist) and Great Britain (liberal).

The empirical basis of the measurement of the structural transformation are the suppliers and the supply of the thirty largest newspapers and current affairs magazines ("general interest outlets with political focus") for 1960, 1970, 1980, 1990 and 2005 and of the thirty largest news and current affairs programs (television) for 1990, and 2005.

In view of differentiation theory, we analyze the (growing) degree of differentiation of the media from their former social and political ties by capturing and categorizing the structure of media suppliers, expecting different types of (selection and interpretation) logics and orientations (citizens or consumers) depending on the type of suppliers (public service, intermediary, economic). Along with this analysis of the functional dimension of differentiation, we also capture the stratificatory dimension of differentiation (cf. Hallin/Mancini 2004; Imhof 2006) focusing on the dominance (or power) of media suppliers and media supply. Our proposed indicators measure the degree of media concentration on the one hand, and, by categorizing newspapers and current affairs magazines into (1) popular/tabloid press, (2) forum/'serious' press or (3) quality press, the dominance of certain media formats and media supply on the other hand. Television programs are categorized into (1) soft news, (2) mixed, or (3) hard news. This method and categorization allows us to show the structural change in a cross-country and diachronic comparison. Below, we can provide preliminary results from this analysis.

Essential Findings

First results from our project show that in Western-style democracies, the press has disentangled itself from their former social and political ties. This process is most striking in the small, democratic-corporatist states (Austria, Switzerland) but not linear in a polarized-pluralist state (France). Furthermore the increasing importance of tabloid media is a phenomenon affecting all countries but to differing degrees.

Figure 1 shows the development of the structure of suppliers of the thirty largest general interest titles with a political focus in Austria, Germany, Great Britain and Switzerland (data for France is work in progress).

Figure 1: Structure of Suppliers – Differentiation of the Press from its Environments – Intermediary Suppliers

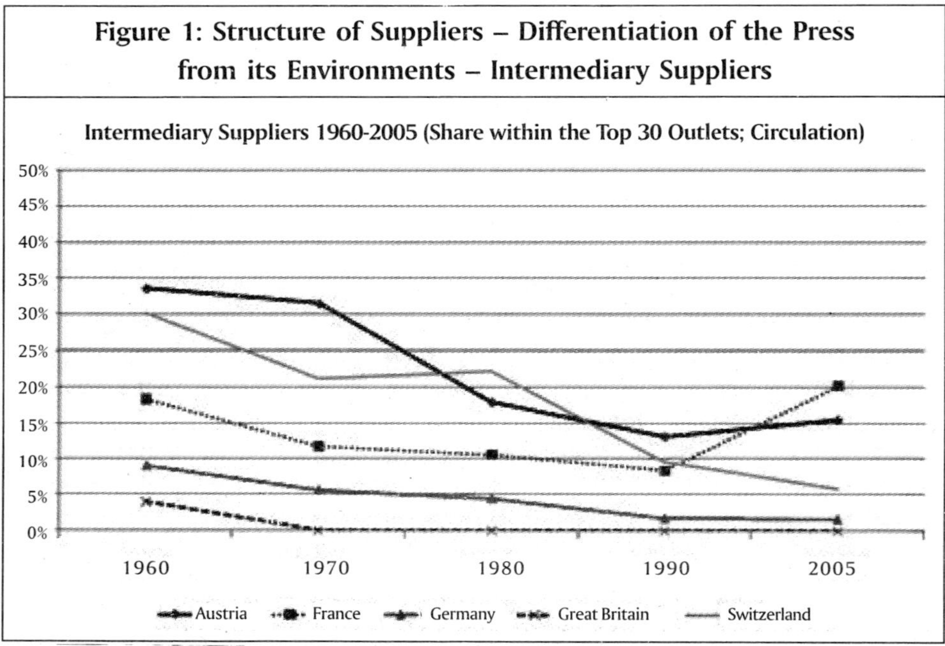

The analysis clearly shows the process of 'disembedding' of the press, most strikingly in press systems of the democratic-corporatist model. Especially in Germany and Switzerland, the press has disentangled itself from their former social and political ties, as suppliers now almost exclusively are private businesses (economic). In Austria, the same process can be observed but stronger structural intermediary links remain than in Germany or Switzerland. France saw a disembedding of the press from 1960s on but, more recently, a (temporary) lack of differentiation from political actors (e.g. political mandate of Dassault). Great Britain, on the other hand, only had a (weak) intermediary press 1960, with economically shaped suppliers dominating the press market ever since.

Despite the (positive) result of differentiation of the media from its political and intermediary environments, there is reason to assume that the public sphere is challenged (if not "colonized") by market imperatives (Habermas 2006). Two possible indicators of this are a growing media concentration and a growing number or influence of the tabloid media (which typically are targeted at large audiences to generate the revenue). Both are supported with our data.

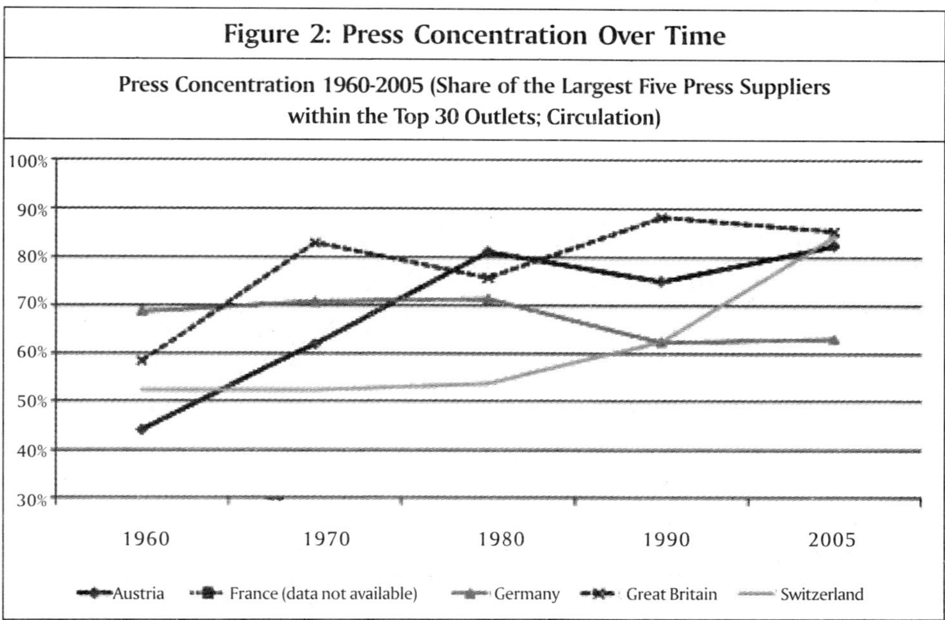

Figure 2: Press Concentration Over Time

Similar to the "disembedding" of the press, press concentration is – comparatively speaking – high already in 1960 in the liberal model (Great Britain) and in the large state of the democratic-corporatist model (Germany) whereas the small states of the democratic-corporatist model (Austria, Switzerland) experience a press concentration later but rapidly. Especially for Switzerland, this process is remarkable, with press concentration becoming a main issue only after the 1980s.

The (overall growing) press concentration we can see in our data often stands in tandem with a (growing) supply of the popular/tabloid press (Figure 3), together indicating the economization of the press. A strong "tabloidization" can be seen in Austria and Great Britain, whereas the popular press plays a slightly smaller role in Germany and Switzerland (according to circulation rates) and a significantly smaller role in France (cf. also Adam/Berkel/Pfetsch 2003). What is crucial, however, is the development of the popular press in the course of time. Here, the small countries within the democratic-corporatist model (Austria, Switzerland) both experience a tremendous growth of the popular press. Great Britain and Germany, whose press outlets have been disembedded for a longer period of

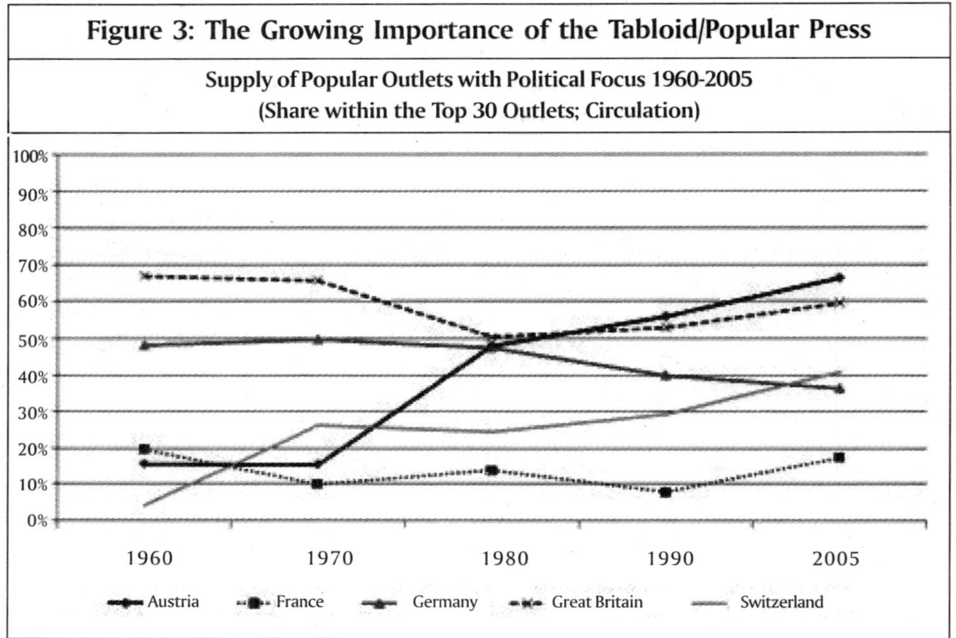

Figure 3: The Growing Importance of the Tabloid/Popular Press

time, also have had a fairly strong popular press but for these countries, the assumption of a growing "polarization between prestige and mass newspapers" (Curran 2000) is probably overstretched, especially for the case of Germany (strong "forum" papers). The press system of France, finally, turns out to be remarkably stable, if we only look at the supply of popular, forum or quality outlets.

These findings, though, have to be interpreted against the background of a television sector where 'soft news' have come to play an increasingly important role. It is true that in Germany (cf. also Lucht 2006), Switzerland, Austria and France, the programs with a high degree of 'hard news' (still) dominate (mainly in public service broadcasting), while political information programs in Great Britain, also those of the BBC, reflect a slightly different concept of information and display more elements of human interest and emotionalizing, thus resulting in a higher number of programs that could be categorized as a mixture of 'soft news' and 'hard news'. But as regards the development over time, our preliminary results suggest a growing 'tabloidization' at the expense of clear hard news formats in all sample countries.

Effects on Political Communication?

All in all, we expect that this increasing commercialization leads to a diffusion of "media logics" into political communication as a whole. This means:

- rising chances of resonance for those actors who adapt to the media logics (especially populist parties) (e.g. Mazzoleni 2008).
- more disclosing and scandalizing in public communication a) over time and b) especially in those media systems where both the supply of popular papers and 'soft news' or mixed programs is high.
- increasing personalization and privatization of political actors a) over time and b) especially in those media systems where both the supply of popular papers and 'soft news' or mixed programs is high.

To answer the hypotheses about the effects of changing media structures on political communication (the content side), we have started conducting content analyses in the summer of 2008 by analyzing one quality, one forum and one tabloid paper each in each of our sample countries, from 1960 to 2005.

(Jens Lucht is the Head of Policy Research Field, Centre for Research on the Public Sphere and Society (fög), University of Zurich. The author can be reached at jens.lucht@foeg.unizh.ch

Linards Udris lic. phil. General in history, is Assistant Professor in the public research sector and society (fög) of the Institute for Science and Media Research (IPMZ) and the Socio-logical Institute (IIP) of the University of Zurich. The author can be reached at linards.udris@foeg.unizh.ch).

Youth Involvement in Democracy Through Internet

Democratic participation requires citizens of the country to be very well informed. Educating the students and the youth about democracy goes a long way in creating an active citizenry in a democracy. Youth involvement is a practice through which the youth can make a difference by having an opinion and sharing control over the decisions and resources that impinge on them. Researches and studies indicate that the young people who take to technology so swiftly will be easily facilitated by new communication technologies. They can empower themselves with knowledge of how a democracy works and how to make it work and form opinions about civic/ public affairs. Amongst the new technologies, Internet is the best way to involve the youth in the democratic process of the country. This form of communication technology provides the youth the opportunity to get engaged and at the same time be aware of the process of decision-making in a democracy. The internet also provides a base for the youth to be a part of various socio-economic development programmes (like education, health and employment) in a country.

Some of the advantages of youth involvement in a democracy through Internet are:

- Internet works as a dais for the youth to discover their own potentials.
- Involvement of youth through internet helps them to acquire and sharpen communication and debating skills.
- Internet also helps in encouraging the young generation to be proactive and being creative for the services they are using in a democracy. In this way the youth instead of being passive can actually become active agents for social change.
- Online games and debates on internet make the youth participation in a democracy more exciting.
- There are a number of websites like Youth Action Net (*www.youthactionnet.org*), Voices of Youth (*www.unicef.org/voy*) and Global Youth Connect (*www.globalyouthconnect.org*) which help in initiating the process of youth involvement in democracy.

The contribution by the young population in a democracy is very vital for its functioning. It is necessary to recognize the chances offered by the, internet to participate in the democratic political system.

(Compiled by Shikha Singh, Senior Research Associate, Icfai Research Centre, Ahmedabad.)

7

Media and Judicial Activism

Shikha Singh

In a democratic system media and judicial activism play a very significant role in highlighting and providing a solution to various socio-economic issues and doing justice for one and all. Both (Judiciary and the Media) are active players when it comes to public activism. They feel it is their intrinsic duty to take up the cudgels against something wrong in society. The article looks at the issues involved in a media judiciary interface; and how adverse court orders do not become activism, nor does a media campaign always become activism and role of media as a catalyst for providing information for socio-economic and political issues. It also looks at the manner in which media and judiciary help in protecting democracy.

Introduction

Democracy can be defined as a system where the people have the right to exercise their voting power to choose their representatives which legislates and empowers a state. "In such a system there is the presence of a representative legislature, regular and timely elections, and enactment of laws through an independent judicial system and the people enjoy universally recognized freedom (political, speech, press etc) and liberties."[1] Also in such a democratic system the media and the judicial activism play a very significant role in highlighting and providing a solution to various socio-economic issues and doing justice for one and all.

Let us now have an insight into what comprises judicial activism. The term judicial activism emerged in India in 1893. It is not a separate concept from the regular judicial activities. To put it differently "judicial activism is a 'blood-cell' of the Judiciary."[2] It is just a new and extended aspect of the judicial analysis. The phrase judicial activism is explained in Black's Law Dictionary, (1891-1991) as, "Judicial philosophy which motives judges to depart from strict adherence to judicial precedent in favour of progressive and new social policies which are not always consistent with the restraint expected of appellate Judges. It is commonly marked by decisions calling for social engineering and occasionally these decisions represent intrusions in the legislative and executive matters."[3] The very essence of true judicial activism is rendering of decisions which are in tune with the temper and tempo of the times. In a similar way we can define media activism as the process of using new communication technologies and media for various social and political issues. It can be related to gathering and spreading information about the social issues and at the same time publishing them in newspapers, on websites, radio, television, movies and the Internet. Both media and judiciary are active players when it comes to public activism. They feel they are duty bound to take up the cudgels against something wrong in society. Hence, it so happens that the judiciary sometimes takes cues from media investigations and takes up Public Interest Litigation (PIL) and sometimes, the media takes a cue from a judgment and goes to town with an agenda of its own. Both media and judiciary join on and off to provide justice to the general public. At large the article looks at the role of media and judiciary in a democracy and the issues involved in the media and judiciary interface and how adverse court orders do not become activism, nor does a media campaign always become activism. It also looks in the manner in which media and judiciary help in protecting the democracy.

---

1 *http://www.pak-times.com/2008/09/04/role-of-indian-judiciary-in-evolution-of-indian-democracy/*

2 *http://mshrc.maharashtra.gov.in/Speech/upload/file%2050.pdf*

3 Ibid.

The Role of Media in Democracy

Media plays a very significant role in supporting a healthy democracy as access to information is very much essential for a democracy to function. Media is the backbone of a democracy, thus providing information in the interest of the general public. Whether it is the Union Budget every year or a change in the interest rates by the Reserve Bank of India (RBI), or attack on the World Trade Tower, or a theft in the neighborhood or a murder of a girl named Aarushi in Delhi, or terrorist attack on the Taj Hotel in Mumbai, or a plane crash: dead and the surviving at Amsterdam's Schiphol airport, it is the media which informs us in the first place. It is only through media, that we become aware of the various socio-economic and political issues around the world. "It is like a mirror, which shows us or strives to show us the bare truth and harsh realities of life."[4] In a country like India where the media is independent, the role extends beyond and enters into the activities like that of anti-corruption and people's participation. Media in a democracy not only informs about the happenings around us but also keeps a close watch over the proceedings of the courts and the judicial decisions.

The Role of Judiciary in a Democracy

For a democracy to function smoothly, it is essential that the courts play their important and influential role. "Courts are government institutions that settle legal disputes and administer justice. Courts resolve conflicts involving individuals, organizations and governments. All courts irrespective of type and jurisdiction are presided over by the judges."[5] "The constitution provides for the establishment of Magistrate Courts, High Court of state, the Court of Appeal, Federal High Court, Sharial Court of Appeal of a state, Customary Court, Election Tribunal, Rent Court, Juvenile Court and the Supreme Court."[6] All these courts have their powers, duties and jurisdiction as laid down by the Constitution and vary from country to country.

The Indian Judiciary has made efforts to support the democratic values of the country over many decades. An example where the courts have defended the democratic principles was in the case of the Nehru government's land reform

---

4 *http://upscportal.com/civilservices/essay/An-Essay-Role-of-media-in-a-democracy*

5 *http://searchwarp.com/swa131887.htm*

6 Ibid.

legislation. This was strongly decided in favor of the fundamental right of right to property, as laid down by the constitution. "The judiciary in modern legal states thus plays very important roles. Apart from ensuring legality, it is obliged to protect against the infringement on the rights and liberties of people by abuse of power by the state and to uphold democracy."[7]

Issues Involved in Media and Judiciary Connection

In a democracy, media and judiciary connection succeeds in providing relief and justice to the public through their joint efforts. In some cases, it so happens that the matters are not taken care of by the judiciary or there is a delay in the process of judgment. At this time media steps in and brings into light the public opinion. At times media is also successful in forming an opinion for the judiciary. This has happened so many times as seen in Rajeev Nanda BMW case, Belgaum case, or the case of a 40-year old pregnant woman with two children on the street of Kerala being beaten up by the people. Another example wherein media activism helped the judiciary to take a decision was in case of Students Islamic Movement. Media highlighted its activities through its various sources of communication like newspapers and news channels, and finally the judicial decision came; it was banned in India.

At times it has so happened that the public on the basis of the media reports has filed the PIL for the weaker and under-privileged sections of the society and the judiciary has taken actions on that basis, after verifying the facts. Hence media as well as the judiciary work to safeguard the rights of the general masses in a democratic set up, helping in nurturing of the democracy.

Thus, judicial and media activism is increasingly coming on the radar of public life, and though we tend to celebrate it, it addresses only a symptom of the deep malaise in society.

But this may not always hold true. "The Indian judiciary is still active to its social responsibility and accountability to the people of the country. Also it has successfully liberated itself from the shackles of Western thought, exercised its power in an innovative manner for the judicial review and has devised new strategies

7 "The Judiciary and Democracy" by Piyabutr Saengkanokkul, Faculty of Law, Thammasat University, 20 April 2008, *http://www.prachatai.com/english/news.php?id=601*

for the purpose of providing justice to the socially and economically disadvantaged groups"[8]. It has brought a new hope of light and justice for the millions of poor and starved people of India.

Attempting to look at things from a different angle, there have been times when the media has assumed the role of the justice system in the country and taken the law in its own hands. As observed in Honorable Justice Sabharwal case, "The media has no right to have parallel justice system and should mind its business. If Sabharwal has committed any wrong, petition can be filed in competent court to get redress but this does not give right to media to assassinate his character or speak malign about him and malign the judicial system".[9] But at the same time there have been instances where media has reversed its role and kept silent over some issues (like social issues or political issues).

The problems arise when either the judiciary or the media force their 'liberal' views on society to steer the action in a particular direction. And when they do it together they can do immense societal good or harm. It is the same premise with which the encounter cops work with a gun, while media protagonists work with a pen and voice.

Conclusion

For the smooth functioning of a democracy it is essential on the part of the media authorities as well as the judiciary to work in a responsible manner. As the democracies get older they need more nurturing and protection, which are duly provided by media activism. Thus, both media and judiciary play an important role in a democracy, and it is not always essential that the adverse court orders will lead to activism by media, nor does all media campaigns always result in judicial activism. But somewhere we can be sure that when both are (media and judiciary) together in a democracy, it will be justice personified. At the same time it is the duty of the general public to be responsible in commenting on the sensational news delivered by the media in a sensible manner and avoid unwarranted public activism that might hurt the dignity and privacy of people involved in the news.

8 By Fathima Razik Cader, "Heart of the Matter", Daily News, 8th October 2003, The Associated Newspapers of Ceylon Ltd. *http://www.dailynews.lk/2003/10/08/fea06.html*

9 *http://www.hindustan.org/forum/showthread.php?t=3333*

Media and Public Interest Litigation (PIL) in a Democracy

Public Interest Litigation (PIL) is a tool to address citizen's problems which need immediate attention from the courts. Any informed citizen or civil society organization can file public interest litigation for redressal of issues of injustice affecting the common man. Unlike conventional judicial process, PILs receive immediate attention from the courts due to their social nature and content. Hence public interest litigation (PIL) is always used as tool to avail speedy justice on matters of public importance. The Public Interest Litigation was started in India by Krishna Iyer J in 1976 (without assigning the terminology) in Mumbai Kamgar Sabha, for disposing an industrial dispute in regard to the payment of bonus.

Though it is a very significant intervention for the judicial system and for the democracy, much care needs to be taken that it should not be misused for trivial pursuits. PILs are valuable and important method of getting social justice expedited. Public interest litigation is necessary to safeguard the democratic values and the fundamental rights of the citizens of the country. Media play a catalyst role in the entire process by providing information upon which PILs can be filed. Media further supports the redressal of such cases by performing their role in advocacy campaigns and creating public awareness and by following up the issues.

(Shikha Singh is a Senior Research Associate at Icfai Research Centre, Ahmedabad. She can be reached at shikhabirsingh@rediffmail.com).

References

1. Isaac A. Blankson and Patrick D. Murphy, eds., "Negotiating Democracy: Media Transformations in Emerging Democracies" (Albany, NY: State University of New York Press, 2007).
2. Gregg A. Payne, "Structural and Social Forces Restricting Media News Content in Democracies: A Critical Perspective", *Journal of Humanities and Social Science*, Vol. 2, Issue 1, 2008.
3. *http://legalserviceindia.com*
4. *http://www.tehelka.com*
5. "Communication for social change", Mazi-articles.
6. *www.thirdworldtraveler.com/Media_control_propaganda/*
7. *http://www.drishtikone.com/?q=blog/womens-rights-and-activism-indian-judiciary*
8. *http://www.pak-times.com*
9. Murray Gleeson (2008), "The Role of a Judge in a Representative Democracy" *http://www.hcourt.gov.au/speeches/cj/cj_4jan08.pdf*

10. *http://www.pak-times.com/2008/09/04/role-of-indian-judiciary-in-evolution-of-indian-democracy/*

11. "Judicial Activism: A Theory of Judicial Philosophy", by Justice A D Mane, Judge, High Court of Bombay, Bench at Aurangabad. *http://mshrc.maharashtra.gov.in/Speech/upload/file%2050.pdf*

12. "Judicial Activism by Media", by Purushottam, Senior Member of Hindustan Movement, 26th September, 2007.

13. P.S. Chopra and J.K. Chopra (2005), "Political Theory and Indian Politics", published by Unique Publishers, New Delhi.

8

e-Democracy in Australia
The Challenge of Evolving a Successful Model

Jenny Backhouse

This paper examines the current status of e-democracy initiatives in Australia and considers the factors that might contribute to the evolution of a successful model of e-democracy in the Australian context. In particular, it examines whether any analogies can be drawn from the world of e-business which has transitioned from an over-hyped boom and then bust in the early years into a steadier and sustained growth in more recent times. The paper concludes that despite some valiant efforts by e-democracy enthusiasts, we are yet to hit on an e-democracy model that truly engages the Australian populace. Nevertheless, the analogy from e-business suggests that, given the right model(s) and the right environment, it can still be possible to deliver real benefits via e-democracy.

Source: http://www.ejeg.com/volume-5/vol5-iss2/Backhouse.pdf *The article was first published in The Electronic Journal of e-Government, Volume 5, Issue 2, pp.107-116.*

1. Introduction

The eventual success of e-business initiatives and the corresponding move to online resources and applications in the e-government arena led many to have high hopes for similar online applications that would enhance democratic participation and decision-making and "transform political cultures ...[and] institutions" (Robbin, Courtright *et al.* 2005 p41). To date, e-democracy initiatives in many countries have had mixed success (Flew and Young 2005 pg 1; Coleman and Norris 2005 p8). Certainly, in Australia, there have been no truly engaging initiatives that have achieved mass appeal such as the Amazon book site did in the early days of e-business and that EBay and various movie and music sites have done more recently.

Admittedly, since democratic focus and democratic processes are primarily national rather than global in nature and do not involve entertainment or commercial profit, we cannot expect quite the same sort of profile as the global e-business arena has achieved. Nevertheless, e-democracy in most countries has failed to live up to the expectations of many dedicated proponents. There is a "... paucity of convincing empirical evidence that ICTs have altered political life" (Robbin, Courtright *et al.* 2005 p417). This is certainly the case in Australia. It is instructive to consider why this might be. Is the concept itself flawed or have we just failed to find the right model(s)?

2. Australia's Political Environment

Australia is a federation comprising six states and two territories. The Australian political climate is fairly stable and largely conservative in its structure and processes (Chen, Gibson *et al.* 2006). There are three tiers of government: federal, state/territory and local. At the federal level and in most state and territory jurisdictions, two major parties are dominant. The structure of the political system at the federal level and in most states means that it is rare for independents or representatives of minor parties to be elected to the single-member electorates in the lower houses, the key legislative bodies in Australian parliaments. At the federal level, the Senate (the upper house) operates as a house of review. Since it is elected by proportional representation from each of the states, minor parties have a better opportunity to get candidates elected to the Senate and they have, on occasion, held the balance of power between the two major parties, thus allowing them more clout in the decision-making process.

Australia has a representative democracy so citizens' influence on decision-making is indirect. One salient feature of Australian governments over the last few decades has been the increased tendency for policy to be decided at the executive level (Chen, Gibson *et al.* 2006). Thus many consider that, with the strong party discipline that prevails, parliament itself has been effectively reduced to a rubber stamp for executive decisions rather than a truly deliberative body.

Consequently, from the viewpoint of structure and practice, the Australian electoral system is not seamlessly responsive to evolving public opinion or to the desires of citizens keen to be more involved in decision-making. Those calling for policy review or input to policy development must rely on other, largely informal, mechanisms such as influencing politicians via lobby groups, trade unions or other citizen and organizational groupings; promoting media campaigns or making submissions to the occasional parliamentary committee. Occasionally, in this globalized world, appeals might be made to supra national bodies such as the United Nations and international labour organisations.

Obviously, politicians have feedback on public sentiment via issues taken up by the media and via public polling by media outlets and other polling organisations. Additionally, the major political parties themselves work hard to monitor public opinion via their own private polling on potential vote-changing issues. Since Australian parliaments have relatively short terms (typically 3 years or less), the prospect of the next election is never far away. Recently, the current prime minister reversed his position on the issue of climate change ("not proven" to "will do something about it") presumably based on awareness that this proposition is now being taken seriously in the electorate.

3. Considering Analogies from e-Business

Despite the initial hype of e-business and the seemingly inevitable bust in 2001, the use of the Internet for commercial purposes has increased steadily and, in some cases, spectacularly. The development of e-democracy models may be informed by considering what factors, if any, affecting the success or otherwise of e-businesses may be pertinent to the development of e-democracy.

3.1 Environment

In the last few years, researchers in the world of e-business have identified some of the necessary preconditions and drivers that contribute to success in e-business (Chaffey 2006). These include appropriate communications infrastructure, government regulatory frameworks, the nature of the business model, readiness of the population to engage in the process (motivation, trust, ease of use, availability of tools, etc). Similar factors could influence the success of e-democracy initiatives.

3.2 Channels

One component of managing a successful e-business is being aware of the "channels" via which customers access your business. Businesses that kept both a store front and an online presence had to consider whether this would increase sales or whether one business outlet would cannibalize the other. For participation in a democratic sense, this is not a critical issue, since more points of access to government and policy decision-makers means greater flexibility for the citizen to choose their preferred method. From a political activist point of view, it may make sense for citizens to use a variety of access channels. Brett Solomon, the executive director of the activist site *getup.org.au*, considers that a successful activist campaign often involves a blend of different strategies possibly including both traditional tactics (e.g., street marches) and online facilitation (Solomon in Barclay 2006).

From the point of increasing citizen engagement, access channels can be an issue. Several researchers have noted that providing participatory and consultation facilities on government websites mean relying on politicians and administrators to approve and administer these initiatives. At the present time, as Dowe notes "Government administrators and politicians are not interested in using the new ideas put forth as it supposedly means more work and less power" (Dowe cited in Coleman and Norris 2005 p15).

A survey by Kim and Holzer (2006) of bureaucrats in South Korea confirmed that many public administrators do have negative attitudes to citizen engagement in the policy making process. Many officials doubt the capacity of citizens to make such decisions. In fact, some members of the public may have particular expertise in certain areas and be better informed than bureaucrats and also politicians who necessarily have to cover a wide area of expertise (Kim and Holzer 2006). A legitimate criticism by South Korean bureaucrats is that forums may be dominated by narrow interests or be reduced to abuse and haranguing of other forum members. Similar reluctance and doubt has been noted by other researchers (Gualtieri cited in Geiselhart, Griffiths *et al.* 2003). The availability of ICT tools will not automatically engender in the citizenry the motivation and ability to process potentially complex information with an open mind. If the aim of e-democracy is to widen the range of democratic participants, then models will need to be designed carefully to encourage the desired result.

3.3 Disruptive Technology

While the Internet has spurred the creation of new online businesses, it has also undermined the viability of some traditional businesses. Amazon was probably the first high profile online business that literally threatened even well established bookstore chains. Currently newspapers are experiencing an eroding of their revenue base, especially those that rely on classified advertising, a field which is inexorably moving online.

Both Thompson and Crabtree (King 2006; Crabtree 2002) warn that the Internet may be similarly disruptive for democracy. It allows citizens to be removed from their geographical ties; to easily filter views so that they only interact with like-minded people, possibly reinforcing extremist views; to have undue clout via small interest groups perhaps lacking a coherent agenda; to expect direct links to political power and correspondingly quick replies. "In this sense, the Internet could be disruptive to the ideal of a public political space. The stable basis of participatory democracy, the need for something in common to help overcome the things on which we disagree, could be gradually eroded. Politics, the process of getting over these disagreements, could be undermined" (Crabtree 2002 p2).

3.4 Resources

In the early days of online commerce, a business could be sustained with a fairly simple website. For serious online businesses these days, maintaining a sophisticated website and the associated applications and infrastructure, is a significant cost. Customer expectations for functionality, appealing presentation, ease of use and the assurance of privacy have risen.

Citizen expectations for e-democracy participatory services are presumably similar. While many government sectors might be considered to have deep pockets and the appropriate technical expertise, the question arises of justifying the expenditure of public monies on e-democracy projects. The returns from projects designed to increase public engagement are likely to be largely qualitative.

Conversely, where e-democracy sites are set-up and maintained by community interest groups or other non-government organisations, they are likely to be subject to pressures such as financial stress and maintaining the enthusiasm of volunteer staff. "E-democracy projects involve more than set-up costs; it has often proved difficult to maintain them as permanent democratic features" (Coleman and Norris 2005 p18).

The rise of e-business saw new players flood into the online market. Despite some spectacular successes, many online businesses were not sustainable. Over time, the well-established and well-resourced traditional companies have been able to re-establish their position in many market segments e.g., News Corporation's purchase of the social networking site *MySpace.com* (BBC, 2005). Some e-democracy pessimists suggest that a similar situation may result from e-democracy initiatives. Rather than bring new players into the game, it may serve to entrench the access of the traditional political players, the so-called elites, lobby groups and major political parties (Norris and Curtice 2006).

3.5 Disintermediation

Early e-business analysts emphasized the likely role of the Internet in disintermediation, cutting out the middleman or agent thus allowing customers to trade directly with product producers. This certainly eventuated in some areas (Chaffey 2006). For example, many low-cost airlines have succeeded in moving most of their customers to direct online bookings, negating the need for travel agents. Traditional airlines have followed suit by setting up their own online booking systems and eventually removing special pricing deals for travel agents.

While disintermediation has occurred in some instances, it has coincided with reintermediation. A whole new group of e-business intermediaries has arisen and proved effective in assisting online consumers to more efficiently perform desired functions e.g., sites which aggregate available accommodation or find the best deal on a particular product, online stock trading sites, sites for accessing music, search engines, etc.

From the e-democracy point of view, political intermediaries have also arisen in the online world. This is particularly obvious in the activist area where organisations such as *moveon.org* use ICTs to rouse citizens, develop electronic petitions and help elect candidates who support their ideals. In Australia, sites such as *getup.org* perform an analogous function.

In the area of e-democracy participation, forums run independently of government perform a similar role replacing, to some extent, the traditional town meeting. E-democracy models therefore should not just model the direct relationship between citizens and government. As Gronlund notes, "... intermediaries of different kinds have begun to interfere in those relations. This includes both service intermediaries ...and 'democracy consultants'" (Gronlund 2002 p1). He cites, for example, the democratic consultation performed in the town of Kalix in Sweden 2001 which was implemented by a private consultant company Votia Empowerment.

Correspondingly, Caddy sees an enhanced role for intermediaries, such as the BBC, who are trusted, branded and separate from government. "... citizens will look to them for packaging and facilitating the access to information" (in Coleman and Norris 2005 p30).

4. The Nature of Democracy and e-Democracy

There is no definitive definition of the concept of democracy, however the "... basic principles of freedom and direct involvement in one's own self government .." are key (King 2006 p16).

The implementation of democracy varies from country to country. Researchers generally distinguish between broad categories of democracy. Gronlund (2003), for example identifies 'quick', 'strong' and 'thin' democracy. In 'quick,' or direct

Table 1: Factors Influencing the Success of e-Business or e-Democracy

Factors	e-business	e-democracy
Environment	• Need for appropriate infrastructure • Supporting regulatory framework	• Need for appropriate infrastructure
Access channels	• Careful management needed	• Variety of access channels is a plus
Citizen engagement	• Clear motivation – satisfying desires (social, financial, etc)	• Motivation less compelling – citizen reluctance • Prospect of domination by narrow interest groups
Disruptive technology	• New businesses created • Some existing businesses undermined	• Could undermine existing political power structures • May lead to expectations that can't be met (e.g., direct access to politicians)
Resources	• Sophisticated sites require significant resources • Well-resourced companies reestablishing their position	• Resources needed but return largely qualitative • Need to maintain enthusiasm of volunteer community groups • May reinforce position of elites
Disintermediation	• Occurred in some areas (e.g., airlines) but new middlemen have arisen (e.g., sites for finding accommodation)	• Independent forums; sites to coordinate and motivate political activism • Democracy consultants; trusted brands

democracy, the citizen makes decisions by responding to opinion polls and representatives are bound by those decisions. An example is the Citizen Initiated Referenda in the Californian context.

Thin, or representative, democracy means the citizen's role is as a voter and the representative, once elected, is given an open mandate for decision-making. As Bishop notes, representative democracy "is often disparaged as not 'true' democracy" and considered to distance citizens from their political representatives and the decision-making process (2002 p39). In contrast, strong or deliberative democracy, entails the citizen being included in open debate and the representative, after election, continuing to interact with the citizen about decisions.

The primary drivers for e-democracy initiatives globally have been both the prospect of taking advantage of the opportunities provided by technical developments in Information and Communications Technology (ICT) and the perceived need to raise the level of citizen participation in the democratic process, particularly as evidenced by factors such as declining voter turnout at elections in many democratic countries (Gronlund 2003). Proponents of a more direct or deliberative and participatory model of democracy therefore see ICTs as an opportunity for this 'truer' form of democracy that will "reinvigorate involvement in the public sphere" (King 2006 p18). Taking a broad view of this reinvigoration, e-democracy includes the use of ICTs not only by governments at all levels but also actors such as political parties, the media, citizen groups and lobby groups (Clift in King 2006).

5. Developing e-Democracy Models

Democracy and decision-making are multi-dimensional, so there are a variety of approaches that may help identify a role for e-democracy initiatives. The nature of the democracy is one factor that impacts on the role of ICTs in the models of e-democracy developed (Norris and Curtice 2006).

Democratic governments typically follow a decision-making cycle consisting of agenda setting and analysis followed by creating, implementing and monitoring the policy (Macintosh 2004; Gronlund 2003). These stages are relevant for e-democracy models since, as Gronlund discusses (2003), the extent of the role for public participation depends on both the broad category of democracy (e.g., thin, strong) and the stage of the decision-making process. In the case of strong democracy, citizens could be involved in all stages whereas, in thin democracy, their involvement is likely to be confined to the policy creation stage and possibly, the policy monitoring stage.

King (2006 p28) presents a different categorisation for identifying aspects of democracy which may be addressed by e-democracy.

- Anticipatory democracy: informed guiding of future decisions
- Deliberative democracy: debating and analysing potential policy
- Grassroots democracy: emphasizing small local initiatives

- Participatory democracy: consensus decision-making and resolving disagreement
- World democracy: informing world-wide movements.

Some authors characterize e-democracy as a more mature stage of e-government. Riley (cited in Shackleton, Fisher *et al.* 2004 p3), for example, identifies three stages of e-government maturity: e-government, e-governance and e-democracy. Shackleton and others, however, counter that e-democracy is not simply a progression from earlier stages of e-government and that the stages, and therefore models, may vary in different levels of government (Shackleton, Fisher *et al.* 2004). Additionally, e-democracy, using the broad definition, is not the sole prerogative of government since other outside actors are involved.

Several researchers have highlighted the multi-dimensional nature of e-democracy in the wider context of society. Parvez (2006) for example, identifies the technological, institutional and agency dimensions that impinge on implementations of e-democracy. The technological dimension includes factors such as access to information resources and the ability to participate in online discussions. The organisational dimension includes factors such as policies and procedures, available resources and institutional attitudes. The agency dimension includes factors such as the nature of e-democracy participants and the difficulties they encounter and attitudes of individuals (e.g., citizens, politicians).

Building on the structuration theory of Giddens and earlier work by Orlikowski, Parvez (2006) has developed a comprehensive framework which provides an approach for explicitly recognizing and examining this multidimensionality of e-democracy and the interaction between these dimensions. His double-structuration loop (Parvez 2006 pg 336) acknowledges the dual roles of technology-shaping processes and technology-use processes and how human actors interact with these. The inner loop, technology-shaping processes, examines "how technological infrastructures that support e-democracy projects evolve and are shaped in an ongoing process by human actors". The outer loop, technology-use processes, examines "how human actors interact with technological infrastructure ...... to enact e-democracy practices and engage in the democratic process". See Figure 1.

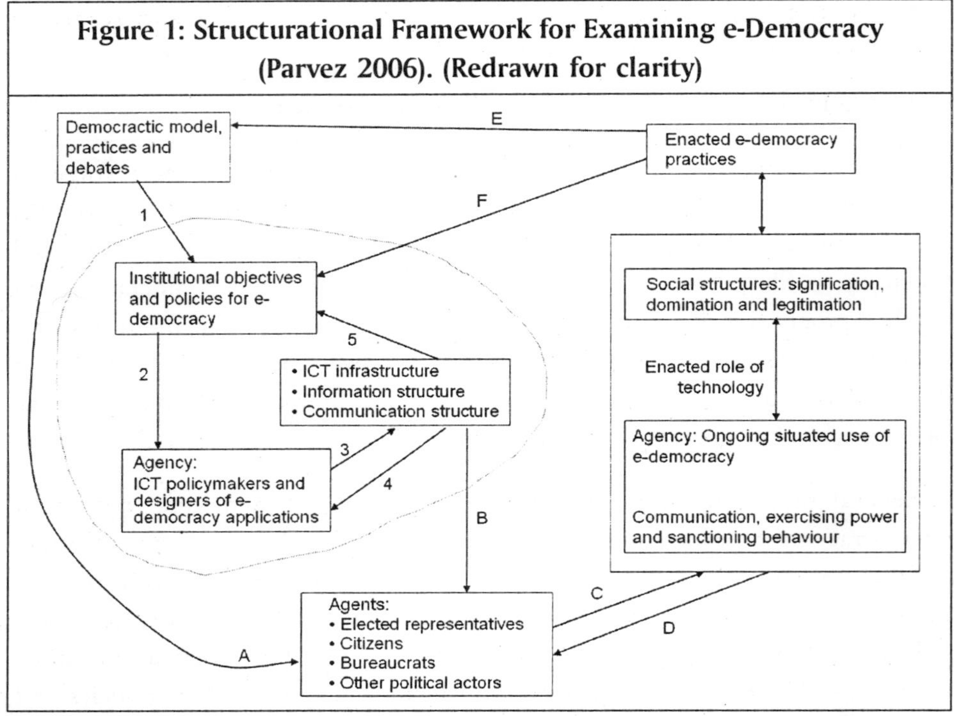

Figure 1: Structurational Framework for Examining e-Democracy (Parvez 2006). (Redrawn for clarity)

This framework provides a useful approach for reflecting on the different aspects of e-democracy. It recognizes the enablement and constraints that social and political actors encounter interacting with the technological and political environment.

6. The Australian Perspective for e-Democracy

6.1 e-Government Progress

Over the last several years, Australia, like many other countries, has implemented a variety of systems, at both state and federal level, to provide government information and transactional services online. These online government services have matured so that Australia was ranked 6th in the United Nations e-Government Readiness Index of 2005 (UNPAN 2005). The Australian Government Online Directory (GOLD) was noted as an example of a best practice portal for finding government information online.

e-democracy however, requires more than just information and service delivery. It requires facilities whereby the citizenry can be more involved in the actual decision-making process, through consultation and the ability to discuss and deliberate on government policy proposals.

6.2 Infrastructure

In terns of access, Australia has been relatively slow in improving Internet infrastructure and the price has remained relatively high, especially when compared with other developed countries. This is particularly the case in the lower-density rural and remote areas (King 2006). It is only recently that the proportion of broadband users has surpassed the proportion of dial-up users online (OECD 2006). While this does not directly impinge on participation, a faster and possibly "always on" connection certainly makes such participation easier. The technological base of e-democracy needs to ensure that we allow equality of access; ease of use; ability to process the information provided so that we do not deepen the digital divide that is already evident (King 2006).

6.3 Disengaged Citizenry

In the Australian context, voter turnout, as such, is not indicative of citizen apathy since voting in elections is compulsory at both the state and federal level. Nevertheless, claims of political disengagement among the populace have been widespread in academic, media and journalistic circles (Goot 2002; King 2006). Such claims typically cite characteristics such as increased distrust of both politicians and the political process, falling membership of political parties and trade unions and young people not registering for the electoral roll. According to the political scientist Jaensch "… the 'main component' of Australian political culture has long been 'a combination of apathy towards politics, and a scepticism, even a cynicism, towards its institutions and political actors'" (cited in Goot 2002).

Goot (2002) himself disputes the extent to which this is a new phenomenon and provides some evidence that citizen engagement has varied over time depending on the political circumstances. Nevertheless, he does find that the attachment to political parties has waned and that voters are increasingly cynical about election promises and doubtful of the honesty and ethical character of politicians. Thus, in Australia as elsewhere in the democratic world, there is still the need to encourage an informed and engaged citizenry if, as claimed by many, this is required to reinforce the legitimacy of government and ensure a vibrant democracy (Bishop 2002 p41).

6.4 Current Assessment

The democratic Audit of Australia assesses Australia's position as a democracy using questions from IDEA (the International Institute for Democracy and Electoral Assistance). The recent review (Chen, Gibson *et al.* 2006) focused particularly on the role of ICTs in the Australian democratic process and in citizen participation. The audit findings indicate that political parties and governments have been slow to take up opportunities to augment citizens' participation. These findings lend support to the view that technologies, of themselves, are not sufficient to promote enhanced opportunities for political engagement. The general conservatism of the Australian political structure and culture also plays a part.

In the audit, ICTs are seen to have had both positive and negative effects. There have been some initiatives designed to open up democratic practices. For example, the researchers (Chen, Gibson *et al.* 2006) identify:

- innovations by political parties, especially minor parties, that serve to improve the visibility of their operations
- new technologies being made more generally available and accessible
- online applications that permit citizens to critique policy development.

Correspondingly, some changes have served to constrain democratic processes:

- ICTs being increasingly used for surveillance of citizens and their actions
- ongoing lack of appropriate resources at the grassroots level
- downplaying the value of direct interaction between citizen and government
- lack of interest in the general community in taking advantage of those opportunities that are available.

The main political parties in Australia have all had established websites for ten or more years. As discussed in the democratic audit (Chen, Gibson *et al.* 2006), these sites are still used primarily for information provision, rather than engagement, and the target audience seems essentially confined to party members and a limited number of the political elite. Additionally, the limited use of these sites by members of the public means that party interest has waned. Smaller parties are having some success with the greater reach a web presence allows them.

The United Nations E-participation Readiness Index ranks Australia 9th with the comment that "... formal consultation facilitation has previously been Australia's deficit [but] its inclusion on ministry sites now indicates a strengthening of participatory initiatives" (UNPAN 2005 p63). However this facility is quite minimal and, in many cases, perfunctory. The initiatives that do occur on government sites are often smaller low-level projects targeted at specific disadvantaged groups and thus shielded from political flak (Chen, Gibson *et al.* 2006).

In terms of politicians' personal websites, the major parties are imposing tighter constraints to ensure that they follow the party line. Quite recently, one federal member (a leader of the Opposition at the time) allowed members of his electorate to vote online on various propositions put forward on his personal website. However, this facility was quickly removed when the voting ran counter to party policy (Chen, Gibson *et al.* 2006).

Most state governments have developed community websites but these are not aimed at encouraging participation. Sites such as CommunityBuilders in New South Wales provide information, news about local issues and the ability to contact bureaucrats. The state of Queensland has made the most high profile effort with their GetInvolved site that includes online discussions on selected topics and the ability to send e-petitions to parliament (Chen, Gibson *et al.* 2006).

Different tiers of government obviously have different responsibilities and consequently different relationships with citizens. "National governments, responsible for the welfare of a whole country, are unlikely to understand the needs of communities in the same way as local government" (Shackleton, Fisher *et al.* 2004 p9). Therefore many e-democracy researchers see the local government level as the most natural place for government to engage with citizenry (Gronlund 2002; Philipsborn in Coleman and Norris 2005). This is less likely to be the case in the Australian scene since local governments lack real political power and are chronically under-funded being reliant on state government funding for non-routine projects. Not unnaturally, those online initiatives that are promoted tend to concentrate on e-government service delivery, primarily as a means of reducing costs or basic information provision e.g., minutes of council meetings (Shackleton, Fisher *et al.* 2004). There are some exceptions, such as Darebin City Council's consultation forums (Bailey, 2006).

The major political parties do make use of ICTs behind the scenes. They maintain comprehensive databases of voters along with relevant personal information such as contacts they have had with their member of parliament, issues of interest, etc. These allow the local member to use mass mail outs to tailor political messages to particular segments of his/her electorate. The lesser resources of the minor parties means that they cannot compete on the same level. The ability to use ICTs to closely monitor an electorate can be a big advantage in the Australian system, where a relatively few marginal electorates often decide the government.

Many citizen groups and non-government organizations have established websites. These are typically largely static sites providing information and group news. The Australian government has not been proactive in supporting such organizations in their online efforts. Some of the larger organizations are, however, starting to translate their online social capital into political influence. The Australian Council of Social Service, for example, enables site users to send personalised email to appropriate parliamentarians (Chen, Gibson *et al.* 2006). A variety of social commentary or activist sites have arisen. Some of these are transient, being devoted to single issues or particular election campaign issues. The Wilderness Society, for example, had a site for the 2004 election.

The successful sites illustrate that it is possible to engage citizens online and counteract, to some extent, the concentration of Australian media in the hands of a few large organisations. The e-journal *On Line Opinion* provides a forum for the discussion of social and political issues. It is run by a non-profit organisation and works with other organisations (universities, NGOs, trade unions, etc) to provide research into pertinent issues. It is achieving some prominence having made submissions to a recent government health enquiry and subsequently realized visibility with the mainstream media (Chen, Gibson *et al.* 2006).

The activist site *getup.org.au* is broadly modelled on the successful *moveon.org.* Getup has discussions on selected topics. It sends out email to members periodically alerting them that certain decisions are about to be made on particular issues, so that appropriate politicians can be contacted. Brett Solomon of getup, claims some success for one of their recent campaigns when an unpopular bill relating to refugees was withdrawn by the government shortly before a vote was due (Barclay 2006).

Recently, as Australia approaches a federal election (likely to be held before the end of 2007), the role of the Internet and particularly the social networking sites have achieved some celebrity. The Prime Minister's first foray into online video, via YouTube, was to launch his government's policy on climate change. The launch video was widely covered in the traditional media although it was also criticized for being too static and quickly became the subject of spam, abuse and comedic routines (Age, 2007). As has been found elsewhere in the world, this emphasizes the difficulties such technologies produce for politicians in "controlling the message".

Social networking sites enable political actors to have a more intimate relationship with constituents. Along with a specific campaign website, the Australian Leader of the Opposition, like many politicians overseas, has a profile on the sites MySpace and Facebook. How effective this will be, in terms of actual votes at election time rather than just novelty value, remains to be seen. Coleman (ABC, 2007b) suggests "most of what politicians do on the Internet is almost totally ignored". Perhaps, more targeted initiatives are effective. The Prime Minister and the Leader of the Opposition recently took part in a webcast specifically directed at, and restricted to, Christians watching in 700 churches around the country (ABC, 2007a). In an era where the concept of market segments applies also to politics, this initiative attracted an estimated audience of 100,000 people and thus enabled the politicians to more precisely target the Christian lobby.

7. Conclusion

If analogies from e-business and other technological advances are relevant, then it seems that ICTs will impact on democratic processes in Australia whether we wish it or not. ICTs have infiltrated our society and they will have impacts on democracy as in other areas, either dramatic or subtle. The challenge is to learn what lessons we can and ensure that the models developed actually serve to enhance democracy rather than detract from it.

E-democracy is not necessarily a threat to representative democracy. There is plenty of scope to augment the citizen's relationship with government within existing structures. As Crabtree (2003) emphasizes "The political potential of the internet lies not in connecting people to politicians, still less in online voting; it lies in the possibility of bringing citizens together to help themselves".

(Jenny Backhouse, BA, Dip Ed (Sydney), Minf Sc (UNSW), Lecturer and PG Course Coordinator at The University of New South Wales. She can be reached at j.backhouse@adfa.edu.au).

References

ABC, (2007a). "Howard, Rudd woo Christians online". Australian Broadcasting Commission, [online], *http://www.abc.net.au/news/stories/2007/08/10/2001287.htm* (August 2007).

ABC, (2007b). "Politics and the Internet". Background Briefing (transcript) on Australian Broadcasting Commission, [online], *http://www.abc.net.au/rn/backgroundbriefing/stories/2007/1924783.htm#transcript* (May 2007).

Age, (2007). "Howard clip becomes spam magnet". The Age, [online], *http://www.theage.com.au/news/web/howard-clip-becomes-spam-magnet/2007/07/18/1184559838528.html* (July 2007).

Bailey, J. (2006). "Local council e-consultation guide". Australian e-Democracy, [online], *http://democracy.nationalforum.com.au/articles127.html* (February 2007).

Barclay, P. (2006). "Protest in the 21st Century". Australian Broadcast Commission, [online], *http://mpegmedia.abc.net.au/rn/podcast/current/audioonly/ats_20070219.mp3* (19/2/2007).

BBC (2005). "News Corp in $580m internet buy". [online], *news.bbc.co.uk/1/hi/business/4695495.stm* (February 2007).

Bennett, S. and Brennan, S. (2000). "Research Paper No 2". Parliamentary Library of Australia, [online], *http://wopared.parl.net/library/pubs/rp/1999-2000/2000rp02.htm* (February 2007).

Bishop, P. (2002). "Democratic equivocations: Who wants what, when and how?" *Papers on Parliament No 39*, Department of the Senate, [online], *http://www.aph.gov.au/Senate/pubs/pops/pop39/c03.pdf* (November 2006).

Chaffey, D. (2007) *E-Business and E-Commerce Management*, 3rd ed, FT Prentice Hall, London.

Chen, P., Gibson, R., *et al.* (2006). "Electronic Democracy? The Impact of New Communications Technologies on Australian Democracy". *Democratic Audit of Australia: Report No 6*, Political Science Program, Australian National University, [online], *http://democratic.audit.anu.edu.au/papers/focussed_audits/20060809_chen_etal_electr_dem.pdf* (August 2006).

Coleman, S. and Norris, D. F. (2005). "A new agenda for e-democracy". *Forum Discussion Paper No. 4*, Oxford Internet Institute, University of Oxford, [online], *http://www.oii.ox.ac.uk/resources/publications/FD4.pdf* (November 2006).

Crabtree, J. (2002). "Is the Internet bad for democracy?" [online], *http://www.opendemocracy.net/debates/article-8-85-1025.jsp* (November 2006).

Crabtree, J. (2003). "Civic hacking: a new agenda for e-democracy". [online], *http://www.opendemocracy.net/media-edemocracy/article_822.jsp* (November 2006).

Flew, T. and Young, G. (2005). "From e-government to online deliberative democracy". *International Conference on Engaging Communities*, Brisbane, Australia, 15-17 August, [online], *http://www.engagingcommunities2005.org/abstracts/Flew-Terry-final.pdf.*

Geiselhart, G., Griffiths, M., *et al.* (2003) "What lies beyond service delivery – an Australian perspective", *Journal of Political Marketing*, Vol 2, No. 3-4, pp213-233, [online], *www.haworthpress.com/store/product.asp?sku=J199.*

Goot, M. (2002). "Distrustful, disenchanted and disengaged? Polled opinion on politics, politicians and the parties: an historical perspective". *Papers on Parliament No 38*, Department of the Senate, [online], *http://www.aph.gov.au/Senate/pubs/pops/pop38/c02.pdf* (November 2006).

Gronlund, A. (2002) "Emerging infrastructures for e-democracy: in search of strong inscriptions ", *e-Service Journal*, Vol 2, No. 1, pp62-89, [online], *http://muse.uq.edu.au/journals/eservice_journal/v002/2.1gronlund02.pdf.*

Gronlund, A. (2003) "e-Democracy: in Search of Tools and Methods for Effective Participation", *Journal of Multi-Criteria Decision Analysis*, Vol 12, No. 2-3, pp93-100, [online], *http://www3.interscience.wiley.com/cgi-bin/jissue/108069479.*

Kim, C.-G. and Holzer, M. (2006) "Public administrators' acceptance of the practice of digital democracy: A model explaining the utilization of online forums in South Korea", *International Journal of Electronic Government Research*, Vol 2, No. 2, pp22-48, [online], *http://www.idea-group.com/articles/details.asp?ID=6057.*

King, J. (2006) "Democracy in the Information Age", *Australian Journal of Public Administration*, Vol. 65, No. 2, pp16-32.

Macintosh, A. (2004). "Characterizing e-participation in policy-making". *37th Annual Hawaii International Conference on System Sciences*, 5-8 Jan, [online], *http://ieeexplore.ieee.org/xpls/abs_all.jsp?arnumber=1265300.*

Norris, P. and Curtice, J. (2006) "If you build a political web site, will they come?" *International Journal of Electronic Government Research*, Vol 2, No. 2, pp1-21, [online], *http://www.idea-group.com/articles/details.asp?ID=6057.*

OECD (2006). "OECD Broadband Statistics to June 2006". [online], *www.oecd.org/sti/ict/broadband* (February 2007).

Parvez, Z. (2006) "Examining e-democracy through a double structuration loop", *Electronic Government*, Vol 3, No. 3, pp329-346, [online], *http://www.inderscience.com/search/index.php?action=record&rec_id=9602&prevQuery=&ps=10&m=or.*

Robbin, A., Courtright, C., *et al.* (2005) "Policy: ICTs and Political Life", *Annual Review of Information Science and Technology*, Vol 38, No. 1, pp410-482, [online], *http://www3.interscience.wiley.com/cgi-bin/fulltext/111091563/PDFSTART.*

Shackleton, P., Fisher, J., *et al.* (2004). "Evolution of local government e-services: the applicability of e-business maturity models". *37th Annual Hawaii International Conference on System Sciences*, 5-8 Jan, 2004, [online], *http://ieeexplore.ieee.org/iel5/8934/28293/01265308.pdf?isnumber=&arnumber=1265308.*

UNPAN (2005). "Global e-government readiness report 2005. From e-government to e-inclusion". Division for Public Administration and Development Management, United Nations, [online], *http://unpan1.un.org/intradoc/groups/public/documents/un/unpan021888.pdf* (November 2006).

9

Democracy of, in and through Communication: Struggles Around Public Service in Canada in the First Half of the Twentieth Century

Patricia Mazepa

Purpose – In reviewing the application of public service principles in the press, telecommunication and radio historically, the paper aims to identify struggles to develop alternatives that address limitations in state and commercially provided public services across a wide range of communication and cultural practices.

Design/methodology/approach – Taking a political economy of communication approach, a different view of public service is adopted as one that understands service as facilitating the making of communication and culture. The paper uses published and archival sources to identify such examples in Canadian history.

Findings – The paper suggests that the concept of public service has been restricted to thinking in a sender-receiver

Source: The Journal of Policy, Regulation and Strategy for Telecommunications, Information and Media, Vol. 9, Issue 2/3, pp.45-56.

model based on consumption and applied accordingly to different media which has limited potentials for democratic communication.

Originality/value – The paper provides a historical and reflexive view on public service in Canada across media and suggests that public service principles need to be grounded in democracy of, in and through communication as a potential guide to current policy decision-making.

Introduction

The distinction between publishing, telecommunications, and broadcasting is collapsing due to technological convergence: so say the latest Canadian government reports that call for a major overhaul of regulations governing communications that will drive a review of cultural policies (Canada (Government of), 2006; Raboy and Taras, 2004). These times are critical as governments in North America seek to "regulate deregulation" (Hamilton, 2006) in favour of market principles while still ensuring a continued commitment to public service. Given that public service principles have been attached to different forms of communication as if they were distinct or unrelated, a review of how these principles have historically been applied in practice is warranted. As Canada is often seen as one of the models of public service development in communications and culture, and as the first few decades of the twentieth century were foundational, this paper focuses on this time period specifically. It suggests that the concept of public service has generally been understood in terms of a sender-receiver model of communication based on the public's consumption of services. This sees governments or businesses as providers of services to a willing or unquestioning public who consumes the services and registers satisfaction through voting, viewing, listening or buying.

Adopting an alternative view, the paper favours a participatory model which understands public service in terms of facilitating the making of communication and culture as demonstrated historically. It takes a political economic approach that begins with an underlying moral philosophy which holds organizations, whether public or private, accountable to the public good as expressed in concepts such as the public interest and public service (Mosco, 1996). This moral philosophy inextricably links communication and culture with the principles and practices of democracy, that places emphasis on the extent of democratization of communication (in terms of availability and diversity), in communication (pertaining to equitable access and participation in cultural production), and through communication (in enabling inclusive public decision-making) (Hagen, 1992; Hackett and Zhao, 2005). These distinctions are made to clarify the concept of democracy in relation to communication and culture, and to operationalize it both as a method of evaluation and as an objective of practice in providing anchors for public service goals.

Integrating this standpoint with an expanded view of public service permits a historical review of how struggles around public service included a range of means of communication and culture, and opens up considerations of "the public" to the radical and reform activities of labour unions, immigrant organizations, pacifist, educational, and religious groups that have tended to be isolated or excluded from direct policy-making altogether. An examination of these groups reveals an uneven but interlinked movement that advanced a participatory understanding of public service across a broad range of communication and cultural practices involving the press, telecommunications and radio, as well as in areas such as drama and education, among others. In considering these advancements, the paper suggests that such a revised understanding of public service is necessary to inform and ground current policy decision-making.

A Brief on Public Service Contentions

Reviewing the early history of policy-making in Canada indicates a range of extremes in public service development in and around communication and culture. On the one hand, the federal government had made decisions that involved public benefits in a national postal system (1867), in telecommunication through the legislation of a common carrier principle in the Railway Act (1906), and in transportation by nationalizing a network of railways across Canada (1918). Canadian telecommunication historians such as Winseck (1998) following Babe (1990), emphasize that what is most significant about government-regulated communication in these first few decades was how "media" was distinguished and separated between the press, telegraph, telephone, and radio as a result of competition and cooperation between businesses, and related or "retroactive" government regulation, rather than being a result of technological imperatives or democratic public priorities (Winseck, 1998, p. 10; Babe 1990, p. 50). Winseck observes in Canada for example, that attention to apparent corporate public responsibility was the consequence of trade-offs made by businesses in exchange for being granted monopoly-rights. This responsibility was intended to compensate for the supposed failure of market competition, which was otherwise assumed to provide the public with services through competition (Winseck, 1998, p. 10).

While there will continue to be debates as to the extent that public service was a distinct priority of government decision-makers in Canada, telecommunication was nevertheless democratized to the degree that the public was assured – through government regulation – of rights of access by prohibiting "unjust discrimination", of costs through "just and reasonable rates", as well as quality and relative ubiquity of telegraph and telephone services (Winseck, 1998; Ogle, 1979). This view of public service is one which links service to supply in terms of quantity and quality of transmission allowing access providing the public can afford to use it. These decisions integrated an ethical or moral responsibility on the part of corporations and in government regulation that remains part of the blueprint of policy-making today.

On the other hand, while decisions were being made in one part of the federal government to facilitate improved communications access across Canada, during this same time period it also exercised repressive control of communication through acts which made certain communication and cultural practices illegal and dangerous. Unlike the US, wherein the US Constitution guaranteed communication rights such as freedom of speech, assembly and association, the mandate given to Canadians in the British North America (BNA) Act of 1867 made no such provisions. It defined the purpose of Canada's government as responsible for "peace, order and good government" which has largely been interpreted through a conservative ideology that placed the emphasis on law and order. This was evident in 1914 when the government established the War Measures Act which gave the power to Cabinet to establish and enforce any law or policy deemed necessary (in times that the government alone decided were crises) ranging from civil unrest to international war.

Civil unrest was continuous in Canada at this time in the form of labour strikes and anti-conscription and anti-war demonstrations, and government uncertainty compounded to the point where the Liberals and Conservatives joined in a "Union" government (1917-1920) to force through conscription, and enacted legislation that was the official beginning of a "Canadian Red Scare" banning any (suspected) left-wing formations (Keshen, 1996; Kealey, 2000). Building on the War Measures Act, a series of Orders-in-Councils were passed that extended government control over communications – including speech, press, and assembly and association (Schmeiser, 1964, p. 215). This included the institution of a Chief Press Censor's Office, which was enlarged to include telegraph and telephone monitoring, a Censorship Committee, and specific acts that later banned a number of English publications (both foreign and domestically produced) and included all publications produced in "alien" languages (Keshen, 1996, p. 66; Kealey, 2000). A wide range of progressive political parties, labour and working-class identified political and cultural organizations, and their accompanying facilities, activities and publications were thereby declared illegal (complete list in Swyripa and Thompson, 1983, pp. 190-6).

Such actions starkly indicated limitations in government conceptualizations of "the public" as it definitively marginalized or excluded sections of the public due to their differing views and practices of politics, economics and culture. It is in this context that groups and organizations formed to facilitate democracy more generally and devise alternative means and methods of communication that were not otherwise "public". That is, they set out to enlarge the breadth and the depth of political economic and socio-cultural range that addressed the absences and limitations in state or commercially provided public services and (in some cases) circumvented state control on a number of related levels.

On an institutional level, working to enlarge the political democracy in Canada beyond the two-party system, were the independent labour parties, the Communist Party of Canada (est. 1921/1924), and social-democratic political parties such as the Co-operative Commonwealth Federation (CCF) (est. 1933), that each aimed to provide viable alternatives to liberal or conservative versions of political economy and culture (Young, 1969; Abella, 1975; Manley, 1994; Heron, 2000). Immigrant associations such as the Ukrainian Labour Farmer Temple Association (ULFTA) (est. 1925) (Krawchuk, 1996), the Finnish Organization of Canada (est. 1925) (Pilli, 1981; Laine, 1981), and similar smaller organizations had their radical and reformist variants, but their experience with the War Measures Act and the resulting deportations and internments (Roberts, 1988), meant that they had to officially eschew any formal political connections if they wanted to legally exist, and offer or develop any kind of services (Pilli, 1981). Linked to these parties and organizations through their opposition to war and an emerging fascism, were pacifist and religious groups such as the Women's International League for Peace and Freedom (WILPF) (est. 1915) (Boutilier, 1988; Socknat, 1987), the Society of Friends, and the Fellowship for Christian Social Order (est. 1934) (Baum, 1980), as well as youth (Axelrod, 1989), sport (Kidd, 1985; Tester, 1986) and educational groups such as the Workers Educational Association (WEA) which merged as alternatives and in opposition to an undemocratic structuring of politics and culture in general, and worked to provide or facilitate alternatives in communication, beginning with an alternative press.

The Press and Public Service

Communication was democratized on a basic quantitative level as all of these activist organizations produced their own publications (including newspapers, magazines, and pamphlets, etc.) on a non-profit and relatively shared-press basis. This was the "alternative press" of the time (Downing, 2001; Atton, 1999), and they aimed to address the neglect and limitations of public service principles in the commercial press. These principles have to with their basic function as publications (to make public) as well as being underpinned by liberal theory which links "freedom of the press" (a communicative right) to property rights (press ownership). In exchange for this freedom, the press is said to have a social responsibility to the public, and accordingly to provide the public with a service – that of information. In the United States (and later in Canada), newspapers were given preferential postal rates through the federal postal system – which itself became a public service when postal rates were lowered to an accessible range (Smith, 1973; John, 1995). Information via the press was to enable citizen decision-making in government as voters, as well as providing a check on government control, such that the role of the press is one of government "watchdog" (Starr, 2004). This view of public service has been interpreted as being one of aiding the development of a "public sphere" providing access to information for informed decision-making (Syvertsen, 1999; Downey and Fenton, 2003) as was facilitated by the (inter)national postal system (John, 1995).

In critiquing and extending the model of the press as government watchdog, Splichal suggests that the model has neglected a commitment to a normative understanding of "publicity" which he submits has historically carried a moral imperative of "intent" that understands publicity as a "prevention or hindrance of the use of power" (Splichal, 2002, p. 7). In this view, the press is "opposed to the economic sphere and its dominant right of private ownership" rather than subordinated to it (Splichal, 2002, p. 7). In Canada, this latter principle was compromised by the dominant commercial model of the press which was well entrenched by the 1920s (Sotiron, 1992). The commercial press' neglect of power was made obvious when the government established the War Measures Act and the media provided little comment or criticism of its actions (Avery, 1983). Furthermore, newspapers in the major urban centres of Canada demonstrated their own limitations, and powers – both as gatekeeper and agenda-setter – as the Canadian "red scare" was perpetuated in representations of "them" (of the organizations which were made illegal or a whole range of groups that could otherwise be considered "radical") were subsequently lumped together as revolutionaries or subversives (Keshen, 1996; Avery, 1979). Indeed, even after the repeal of the War Measures Act, the Royal Canadian Mounted Police kept vigilance over any suspected "subversive" in regular reports to the federal government (Kealey and Whitaker, 1989-1997). For immigrants in particular, in contrast to the efforts that the Canadian government made in translating brochures and advertisements in their native languages in Europe, no such information and translation was provided once they were in Canada (Pilli, 1981). For these reasons, self-publication was a necessity, and alternative production and distribution networks were made to address such exclusions and to exercise a freedom of the press that went beyond government or commercial limitations.

The largest immigrant organizations founded or supported publishing companies and by the 1930s were able to publish daily additions of their newspaper (Hoerder, 1987a, b; Pilli, 1981; Krawchuk, 1996). This was quite an accomplishment given that some of the large commercial papers did not survive during this time (Kesterton, 1967). Publishing was a cooperative activity as printing presses were shared and funding was provided by the larger organizations to the smaller papers indicating that the alternative papers were not considered "competition" in contrast to the commercial model of the press. Supplementing regular publications, and meant as publicity in terms of exercising a freedom of the press that was not based on private ownership, were the many and frequent flyers, pamphlets, and single broadsheets that were advertised in the newspapers, posted on street corners and in community halls, and distributed by hand in the street as alternative forms of distribution (Weinrich, 1982). These distribution networks ranged from the larger organization levels of the political party press, to the radical bookstores that were its rare but frequent advertisers, to the libraries in the immigrant community centres, to "peace libraries" that were open to the public (Boutilier, 1988, p. 125; Socknat, 1987; Weinrich, 1982). These were complemented by social and cultural networks that developed access and participation around urban and rural spaces of public congregation and in contrast to, and partly due to exclusions from the new technology of the time – the telephone.

Public Networking and Services

Understood in terms of telecommunication, public service is generally considered fulfilled by facilitating access to technology, ensuring "just and reasonable rates" and "common carriage" regulations so that corporations do not discriminate or interfere with the content of messages transmitted along their lines. In this sense, public service is understood as a "public utility" in that its "prime criteria of success are signal quality, efficiency of operations and a distribution network that provides universal access" (Syvertsen, 1999, p. 6). This tends to assume that control over the technology, and the technology itself is neutral, while leaving to debate and negotiation as to what cost can be considered "just and reasonable" (Winseck, 1998). In Canada, before the Railway Act of 1906 (and well into the 1940s), initial costs for fixed or private telephone services were "prohibitive" (Martin, 1991, p. 42), and thus a variety of public services were initiated using multi-point connections.

In the late 1800s, examples of so-called "party-line" connections included the transmission of church services for those who could not physically attend the regular mass such that the broadcasting potential of the telephone was recognized early on (Collins, 1977, p. 81). A range of public services were experimented with including the provision of medical diagnosis over the phone for which the phone companies gave doctors "a cut rate" (Collins, 1977, p. 81). At the turn of the century, group meetings and newspaper reading groups also made use of multiple party lines (Martin, 1991) as did the later provision of adult education classes which laid the foundations for distance education (Armstrong, 1968).

Despite such potentials, however, early telephone access was divided along both social class and gender lines demonstrating an early "digital divide" (Martin, 1991). Rates were set advantageously towards the predominantly business subscribers and to the economic justifications presented by the Bell Canada Company as the monopoly telephone provider in Ontario and Quebec, and was correspondingly priced out of the reach of the working class (Martin, 1991). Thus, how it was developed as a private point-to-point communication, together with its costs, made it less of a social and organizing medium and more of a tool for business (Martin, 1991). Alternative communication and cultural development during this time thus remained based on oral or face-to-face social networks that were more effective in facilitating participation. In the early decades of the twentieth century it was the place rather than the technology that helped facilitated public communication and these included the many community centres or "labour temples" as well as public parks, government grounds, and the streets (Heron and Penfold, 2005).

Central houses, community homes and halls served as political economic and socio-cultural centres for the public in general and for immigrants in particular. While only a few "labour temples" were recorded at the turn of the twentieth century, by the 1930s they were well established both in urban and rural areas. The Jewish halls (in Toronto, Montreal and Winnipeg) were first built to house labour unions and provided them with a centralized meeting place and expanded from there (Frager, 1992). The Labour Lyceum in Toronto was situated at the heart of the garment district and acted as a combination labour college, arts academy and recreation centre meant to complement "the informal socializing at the union halls" (Frager, 1992, p. 40). By the 1930s, the Ukrainian Labour Farmer Temple Association (ULFTA) had over 100 labour temples located in areas of immigrant concentration and of these, the Ukrainian labour temple in Winnipeg was the largest covering a whole city block and containing a "one thousand seat auditorium, administration offices, a school, library, and print shop" (Kisilow, 1986; in Hunchuk, 2001, p. 80). The labour temples provided shelters, drop-in centres, and a general "home-away-from-home" environment and were a hub of organizational and fund-raising activities.

The labour temples also provided a much needed public service since the federal government had ensured immigrants fulfilled their role as able-bodied labour and little was done to assist in language acquisition skills (Eklund, 1987, p. 25). Immigrants were thus expected to fulfill their role as labourers, rather than necessarily participating in decision-making processes as citizens. Activities in the labour temples filled this void. In general, a comprehensive approach was taken to citizenship. This included the development of organizational skills (administration, leadership training, and educational work), communication and media skills (teaching, public speaking, editing and reporting for the press), "cultural work" (plays, writing of poetry, stories, songs, and music) (Krawchuk, 1996; Kolasky, 1979; Patrias, 1994; Frager, 1992; Eklund, 1987). It was this cultural work that further facilitated democracy in communication as the public were drawn to participating in the productions and thus provide classic examples of a different concept of public service.

Making Culture Public

Facilitating public participation in culture involves dismantling dominant practices that replicate the sender-receiver model implicit in public service delivery. Multiple examples from the 1920s and 1930s indicate sustained efforts at reducing political economic and social barriers in activities considered "culture" like performance arts, sport and education (Mazepa, 2003). In performance arts, what came to be known as "social theatre" disrupted the traditional performer-audience division through the play's plot lines and overall organization, and these were part of the plays at the labour temple and were developed through mobile and stationary theatre groups (Wright and Endres, 1976). A standard theme in drama at the labour temples was "everyday life" that did not ignore social relations of class, gender and race, nor take them as a given. Rather, plots focused on class struggle, strikes, the Depression, labour (in the factory and in the household), pacifism and anti-clericism, and addressed them in plays ranging from serious tragedy to farcical acts. In this way, the plays were more likely to instil a sense of participation, not only in the production, but also in what the plays were about. In the mobile and stationary groups, the initial aims were "agit-prop" – a combination of agitation and propaganda – that extended and erased the conventional structures of theatre. This involved altering characters, plot lines, endings, and erasing distinctions between audiences and performers. This distinction was demonstrated in what was called the "mass recitation" where everyone in attendance was encouraged to participate in the plays and vocalize their participation, to symbolize their collective strength and their potential as a social movement (Endres, 1976, p. 8).

As "social theatre" and participation in the plays and clubs grew, however, the terms of success were the harbinger of its own demise. Demands on the size of venue also increased and most of the labour temples and the few alternative theatres were too small to accommodate them such that the venue shifted to the larger and more expensive halls that were restrictive in terms of costs and social status. The venue change was accompanied by a distinction between audiences as spectators, and players as performers, and judgements were made in the commercial press and by trained adjudicators on the basis of hegemonic artistic and technical merits rather than the social and participatory elements. In turn, this separation allowed the "audiences" and "judges" to separate and admire the dramatic elements of the play while criticizing "propaganda" as a negative and undesirable quality of drama (Bray, 1990). This separation was encouraged by the federal government though its involvement in amateur theatre that rewarded technique through the sponsorship of contests at a national level (Bray, 1990). Through the contests, the provincial government became involved in funding of theatre as well and used similar criteria in its organization and support of the development of "community theatre". While the government's resources were a welcomed addition, the emphasis on technique and return to traditional play structures destabilized the social and public emphasis of the movement. Coupled with the beginning of the Second World War, and schisms within groups as to future directions, the social theatre movement came to an end and the division between audiences and performance remained. This division was also evident in the struggles for public participation in and ownership of broadcasting in the 1920s and 1930s.

Public Service Broadcasting

In radio, public service was initially interpreted at the beginning of the 1920s as a technical requirement – having to do with scarcity of signals and interference from other broadcasters whether this was on a local or national level (Johnston, 1992). Empowered by the BNA Act, the federal government regulated the use of these frequencies through the Radio Branch as a matter of jurisdiction through the granting of licenses which distinguished between radio clubs or "amateur" stations and commercial owners or "private stations". Even though radio technology allowed two-way communication, like the telegraph and the telephone, communication was viewed as a matter of transmission between sender and receiver, in this case, between the broadcaster and the listener, which set the framework for legislation and for thinking about "the public" – as listeners.

Although the multi-point transmission made the technology different from the telegraph, initially its content was not a matter of national issue, as it was simply a question of whether the public enjoyed it or not (Johnston, 1992, p. 70). In the late 1920s, regulation became a more political and contentious undertaking as more numerous and powerful signals from commercial stations in the USA were interfering or blocking local Canadian stations, and questions of national sovereignty, economy, and cultural identity, coupled with a fear of American economic and cultural influence, merged and emerged over the control of radio. These arguments became contentious enough for the federal government to create a Royal Commission on Radio Broadcasting (the Aird Commission) (1928) which was followed by the establishment of the Canadian Radio Broadcasting Commission (CRBC) in 1932, and subsequent parliamentary debates on whether the structure of ownership of broadcasting should be private or public, or a mixture of both (Raboy, 1990, pp. 17-47).

Public ownership was supported by a number of ideologically diverse groups including socialist, cooperative, nationalist and conservative groups and principally advanced by an autonomous organization called the Canadian Radio League (O'Brien, 1964; McChesney, 1999) but after seven years of government deliberations, the decisive result was a mixed system as provided in the Canadian Radio Broadcasting Act in 1936. The Act established a "national broadcasting service" the structure of which included the state managed and controlled broadcaster – the Canadian Broadcasting Corporation (CBC) – and private broadcasters that were licensed by the government and either affiliated to American broadcasting companies or independent local stations (Maclennan, 2005). It was accompanied by an idea that the public was to be served by the CBC as "an instrument of nation building" and programming was supposed to reflect a "Canadian" culture and promote unity across geographical, language, social class and cultural differences. Thus, as Raboy (1990) identifies, the public interest was equated to the national interest, and given the existence of socialist political parties, labour unions and immigrant activism, unity was promoted as a way of countering class divisions and social unrest. What this would mean for content, however, has been a subject of continual debate.

The "state-as-broadcaster and the public-as-listener" structure was relatively undisturbed over almost a decade of deliberation, save for several presentations made to the government by the Toronto Musical Protective Association that "upset the balance of the listeners and broadcasters" by introducing a "third element" and bringing questions of labour and cultural production to the fore (Johnston, 1992, p. 70). As a branch of the union of the American Federation of Musicians, the Protective Association had been involved in negotiations and controversies over recorded music and the production of electronic transcripts with private broadcasters and the regulators from the late 1920s into the mid-1930s, but these were largely seen as internal debates rather than parliamentary ones (Johnston, 1992, p. 70). Fundamental questions regarding labour and the production of content had generally been excluded in the sender-receiver model of policy formation. The union appears to be the first organization to advance a Canadian content policy, but this did not make it into the 1936 government regulations (Skinner, 2005), despite a strike by the musicians in 1934 for a closed shop and standard pay scale (Johnston, 1992, p. 93).

Furthermore, recent analyses of the programming in the early years of broadcasting (1930-1939), illustrates that there was limited indigenous or alternative production supported by the CBC. The focus on listeners as audiences, and the position that the CBC took in programming decisions as a competitor in order to attract those audiences, indicates that the CBC actually facilitated the dominance of the commercial model through its purchase and carriage of American programming (Maclennan, 2005). Efforts to advance democracy through communication on radio thus emerged in the form of educational programming and the actions of organizations like the Worker's Educational Association (WEA) (est. 1913), the Canadian Association of Adult Educators (CAAE) (est. 1935), and a number of labour unions affiliated to the national Trades and Labour Congress of Canada (Radforth and Sangster, 1981; Comor, 1987; Faris, 1975).

As the first of these, the WEA took the initial idea behind the elite and British origins of adult education – which was supposed to bring "culture to the labouring man" through a liberal education and indoctrinating loyalty to the Empire – to fashion their motto: "education for citizenship" (Radforth and Sangster, 1981). As the Canadian governments' view of adult education was solely focused on vocational training, the aim was to "democratize education" for citizenship of a more radical, that is, participatory sort. Appreciating the importance of media ownership, the WEA purchased their own film production and exhibition equipment, and "established a film library that was widely used by unions and other organizations" making pioneering developments in the use of film and slides, as well as radio for long-distant classes and promotion of discussion groups (Radforth and Sangster, 1981, p. 65; Comor, 1987, p. 21). Radio was beginning to be used by religious groups and provincial governments as a means of education (Faris, 1975) and in 1937, the WEA launched a Workers' Educational Series on the CBC that had a brief life of nine-programs before it was cancelled due to an official statement of "inferior technical quality" and unofficially due to complaints by business leaders and a continuing "red scare" that identified any such radical ideas or practices as "communist" (Klee, 1995, p. 108).

Other less radical adult education initiatives during the interwar period were promoted by the Canadian Association of Adult Educators (CAAE) which developed from the more elite and traditional model of education aimed at adults in rural areas in particular, but it also used radio and the telephone for long-distance courses (Faris, 1975). In cooperation with the Canadian Federation of Agriculture and the CBC, it established the National Farm Radio Forum (1941-1953) and later the Citizen's Forum (1943-1952) that experimented with two-way communication in community problem-solving and national issues, and was meant to promote national unity (Romanow, 2005, p. 114). The National Farm Radio Forum's formula of "read-listen-discuss-act" was considered a model of participatory radio by UNESCO as it involved participants on a local, regional and national level in a research, discuss and feedback loop that was meant to identify farming challenges, common problems and possible solutions in cooperation with government agencies (Raboy, 1990, pp. 74-77; Romanow, 2005). These programs were very successful in terms of the length of time they remained on the CBC, but continual under-funding, frustration on the part of the participants as to government (in)action on the issues, elite and paternalistic underpinnings, as well as limits to the range of discussion allowed due to government surveillance, tempered its success.

Although ongoing surveillance by the RCMP of any suspected "revolutionary organizations and agitators" had continued with vigilance from the First World War, the government's exercise of control over communication and culture was again made explicit immediately after it declared its entry into the Second World War in 1939. For the second time the government initiated the War Measures Act, and it now banned all spoken-word broadcasting on the public and private airwaves in languages other than English and French (Mazepa, 2003). It set up a new Censorship Committee, the details of which were clarified in subsequent directives that placed limits on all types of news or "talks" that needed be cleared before broadcasts would be permitted which included any talks on "labour and capital" and even the broad content of the Citizen's and Farm Forums. And if the radio censorship did not go far enough, specific newspapers and particular immigrant organizations like ULFTA and the FOC were later banned outright under the Defence of Canada Regulations (Canada, Government of, 1940; Mazepa, 2003).

As was evidenced by the deliberate and sustained actions of the federal government, what was thus developed as "culture" and allowed as "communication" in Canada would include little that threatened the dominant hegemony, and this was exercised most severely in times of war or perceived threat. Nevertheless, this did not mean that public service initiatives and alternatives means and methods ceased to develop; it rather signifies the breadth and the depth of a battle that continues.

Conclusion

The consideration of public service principles as have been applied within liberal democracies are filtered through capitalism in negotiations with the communication and cultural industries which has resulted in a model of public service whereby "the public" is viewed as a consumer of services, communication is considered to be a transmission between sender and receiver, and democracy is subordinated to economic and ideological imperatives. Based on this model, it may make little difference as to whether government or corporations are providing the services, if the public is treated or sees its role as consumers of those services. While there have been distinct regulations that have distinguished between the press, telecommunications and broadcasting, this model has remained dominant across all of them. Struggles around public service have tried to reverse this model by prioritizing democracy of, in and through communication, by understanding communication as inseparable from culture and labour, and by facilitating public participation in the making of communication and culture.

As reviewed in this paper, movements to democratize communication and culture are part of movements to democratize politics and economics more generally. They worked within or bypassed – whether by choice or necessity – public service limitations across a range of communication and cultural practices. While not without their own contradictions and limitations, such efforts to facilitate democracy of communication included the production and distribution of the alternative press recovering normative principles of "publicity" as a prevention or hindrance of power. Democracy in communication involved linking social and cultural networks that were less dependent on access to technology than they were on access to people. This included alternative and oppositional practices of culture and communication that aimed to break the mould of the consumer or sender-receiver model, through dismantling restrictive or predictable structures in performance art and education, and by identifying culture as a product of labour. Democracy through communication was enabled by immigrant organizations and political parties that were formed to advance social democratic politics, as well as being forged through labour union negotiations, and when governments opened up decision-making processes through Royal Commissions and parliamentary committees. On a more specific level, the national radio programs made a crucial addition to the understanding of public service to Read, Listen, Discuss, and Act. Combining democracy of, in and through communication thus suggests a potential basis for communication and cultural policy convergence as one that facilitates public participation and decision-making, as this would really be – a public service.

(Patricia Mazepa is an Assistant Professor in the Graduate Program of Communication and Culture and in the Communication Studies undergraduate program at York University, Toronto, Canada. The author can be reached at pamazepa@yorku.ca).

References

Abella, I. (1975), *The Canadian Labour Movement 1902-1960*, Historical Booklet No. 28, Canadian Historical Society, Ottawa.

Armstrong, D. (1968), "Corbett's House: the origins of the Canadian Association of Adult Educators and its development during the Directorship of E.A. Corbett, 1936-1951", MA thesis, Toronto, University of Toronto, Toronto.

Atton, C. (1999), "A reassessment of the alternative press", *Media, Culture & Society*, Vol. 21 No. 1, pp. 51-76.

Avery, D. (1979), *Dangerous Foreigners: European Immigrant Workers and Labour Radicalism in Canada*, 1836-1932, McClelland and Stewart, Toronto.

Avery, D. (1983), "Ethnic and class tensions in Canada, 1918-1920: Anglo-Canadians and the alien worker", in Swyripa, F. and Thompson, J.H. (Eds), *Loyalties in Conflict: Ukrainians in Canada During the Great War*, Institute of Ukrainian Studies, University of Alberta, Edmonton, pp. 79-98.

Axelrod, P. (1989), "The student movement of the 1930s", in Axelrod, P. and Reid, J.G. (Eds), *Youth, University, and Canadian Society: Essays in the Social History of Higher Education*, McGill-Queen's University Press, Montréal and Kingston.

Babe, R.E. (1990), *Telecommunications in Canada*, University of Toronto Press, Toronto.

Baum, G. (1980), *Catholics and Canadian Socialism: Political Thought in the United States*, 1789-1930, James Lorimer and Company Publishers, Toronto.

Boutilier, B. (1988), "Educating for peace and co-operation: The Women's International League for Peace and Freedom in Canada, 1919-1929", MA Thesis, Carleton University, Ottawa.

Bray, B. (1990), "Against all odds: The Progressive Arts Club's Production of Waiting for Lefty", *Journal of Canadian Studies*, Vol. 25 No. 3, pp. 489-504".

Canada (Government of) (1940), *Defence of Canada Regulations (Consolidation)*, J.O. Patenaude, I.S.O. Printer to the King's Most Excellent Majesty, Ottawa.

Canada (Government of) (2006), *Telecommunications Policy Review Panel Final Report 2006*, available at: *www.telecomreview.ca/epic/internet/intprp-gecrt.nsf/en/h_rx00054e.html* (Accessed 3 November, 2006).

Collins, R. (1977), *A Voice From Afar: The History of Telecommunications in Canada*, McGraw-Hill Ryerson Limited, Toronto.

Comor, E. (1987), *Challenge and Innovation: A History of the Worker's Educational Association*, WEA, Toronto.

Downey, J. and Fenton, N. (2003), "New Media, counter publicity and the public sphere", *New Media and Society*, Vol. 5 No. 2, pp. 185-202.

Downing, J.D.H. with, Ford, T.V., Gil, G. and Stein, L. (2001), *Radical Media: Rebellious Communication and Social Movements*, Sage, London.

Eklund, W. (1987), *Builders of Canada: History of the Finnish Organization of Canada*, Finnish Organization of Canada, Toronto.

Endres, R. (1976), "Plays and politics: an analysis of various models of 20th Century Political Theatre", PhD thesis, York University, Toronto.

Faris, R. (1975), *The Passionate Educators: Voluntary Associations and the Struggle for Control of Adult Educational Broadcasting in Canada, 1919-1952*, Peter Martin Associates, Toronto.

Frager, R. (1992), *Sweatshop Strife: Class, Ethnicity, and Gender in the Jewish Labour Movement of Toronto*, University of Toronto Press, Toronto.

Hackett, R.A. and Zhao, Y. (Eds) (2005), *Democratizing Media: One World, Many Struggles*, Rowman and Littlefield, Lanham,. MD.

Hagen, I. (1992), "Democratic communication: media and social participation", in Wasko, J. and Mosco, V. (Eds), *Democratic Communication in an Information Age*, Garamond Press, Toronto, pp. 16-27.

Hamilton, T. (2006), "Telecom controls partly lifted", *Toronto Star*, 7 April, pp. F1-F2.

Heron, C. (2000), "Labourism and the Canadian working class", in Sefton-MacDowell, L. and Radforth, I. (Eds), *Canadian Working Class History: Selected Readings*, Canadian Scholars' Press, Toronto, pp. 315-41.

Heron, C. and Penfold, S. (2005), *The Workers' Festival: A History of Labour Day in Canada*, University of Toronto Press, Toronto.

Hoerder, D. (1987a), *The Immigrant Labour Press in North America, 1840-1970s*, Vol. 1: Migrants from Northern Europe, Greenwood Press, New York, NY.

Hoerder, D. (1987b), *The Immigrant Labour Press in North America, 1840-1970s*, Vol. 2: Migrants from Eastern and Southeastern Europe, Greenwood Press, New York, NY.

Hunchuk, S. (2001), "A house like no other: an architectural and social history of the Ukrainian Labour Temple, 523 Arlington Ave. Ottawa, 1923-1967", MA Thesis, Carleton University, Ottawa.

John, R.R. (1995), *Spreading the News: The American Postal System from Franklin to Morse*, Harvard University Press, Cambridge, MA.

Johnston, R.T. (1992), "The Origins of Public Broadcasting in Canada Reconsidered: the Radio Branch and Cultural Administration", MA Thesis, Queen's University, Kingston.

Kealey, G.S. (2000), "Spymasters, spies, and their subjects: the RCMP and Canadian State repression, 1914-1939", in Kinsman, G., Buse, D.K. and Steedman, M. (Eds), *Age of Contention: Readings in Canadian Social History*, 1900-1945, Harcourt and Brace, Toronto, pp. 288-304.

Kealey, G.S. and Whitaker, R. (Eds) (1989-1997), R.C.M.P. *Security Bulletins (7 volumes)*, Canadian Committee on Labour History, St John's.

Keshen, J. (1996), *Propaganda and Censorship During Canada's Great War*, The University of Alberta Press, Edmonton.

Kesterton, W. (1967), *A History of Journalism in Canada*, McClelland and Stuart, Toronto.

Kidd, B. (1985), "The Workers' Sport Association in Canada 1924-40: the radical immigrants' alternative", *Polyphony*, Vol. 7 No. 1, pp. 80-8.

Klee, M. (1995), "Hands-off the labour forum: the making and unmaking of national working-class radio broadcasting in Canada, 1935-1944", *Labour/Le Travail*, Vol. 35, pp. 107-32.

Kolasky, J. (1979), *Shattered Illusion: The History of the Ukrainian pro-Communist Organizations in Canada*, Peter Martin, Toronto.

Krawchuk, P. (1996), *Our History: The Ukrainian Labour-Farmer Temple Movement in Canada*, Lugus Publications, Toronto.

Laine, E.W. (1981), "Finnish Canadian Radicalism and Canadian Politics: the first forty years, 1900-1940", in Dahlie, J. and Fernando, T. (Eds), *Ethnicity, Power and Politics in Canada*.

Vol. VIII, Canadian Ethnic Studies Association, Methuen Publications, Agincourt, pp. 94-122.

McChesney, R.W. (1999), "Graham Spry and the Future of Canadian Broadcasting", *Canadian Journal of Communication*, Vol. 24 No. 1, available at: *www.cjc-online.ca*

Maclennan, A.F. (2005), "American Network Broadcasting, the CBC, and Canadian radio stations during the 1930s: a content analysis", *Journal of Radio Studies.*, Vol. 12 No. 1, pp. 85-103.

Manley, J. (1994), "Canadian Communists, Revolutionary Unionism, and the 'Third Period': The Workers' Unity League, 1929-1935", *Journal of the CHA*, pp. 167-91.

Martin, M. (1991), *"Hello Central?" Gender, Technology and Culture in the Formation of Telephone Systems*, McGill-Queen's University Press, Montreal and Kingston.

Mazepa, P. (2003), "Battles on the cultural front: the (de)labouring of culture in Canada, 1914-1944", PhD thesis, Carleton University, Ottawa.

Mosco, V. (1996), *The Political Economy of Communication: Rethinking and Renewal*, Sage, London.

O'Brien, J.E. (1964), "A history of the Canadian Radio League, 1930-36", PhD Thesis, University of Southern California, Los Angeles, CA.

Ogle, E.B. (1979), *Long Distance Please: The Story of the TransCanada Telephone System*, Collins Publishers, Toronto.

Patrias, C. (1994), *Patriots and Proletarians: Politicizing Hungarian Immigrants in Interwar Canada*, McGill-Queen's University Press, Montreal and Kingston.

Pilli, A. (1981), "Finnish-Canadian radicalism and the Government of Canada from the First World War to the Depression", in Karni, M.G. (Ed.), *Finnish Diaspora I: Canada, South America, Africa, Australia and Sweden*, The Multicultural Historical Society of Ontario, Toronto, pp. 19-32.

Raboy, M. (1990), *Missed Opportunities: The Story of Canada's Broadcasting Policy*, Queen's University Press, Kingston.

Raboy, M. and Taras, D. (2004), "The politics of neglect of Canadian Broadcasting Policy", *Options Politiques*, March.

Radforth, I. and Sangster, J. (1981), "A link between labour and learning: the Workers' Educational Association in Ontario, 1917-1951", *Labour, Le Travail*, Vol. 8/9, pp. 41-78.

Roberts, B. (1988), *From Whence they Came: Deportation from Canada 1900-1935*, University of Ottawa Press, Ottawa.

Romanow, P. (2005), "The picture of democracy we are seeking: CBC Radio Forums and the Search for Canadian Identity, 1930-1950", *Journal of Radio Studies*, Vol. 12 No. 1, pp. 104-19.

Schmeiser, D.A. (1964), *Civil Liberties in Canada*, Oxford University Press, Toronto.

Skinner, D. (2005), "Divided loyalties: the early development of Canada's 'single' broadcasting system", *Journal of Radio Studies*, Vol. 12 No. 1, pp. 136-55.

Smith, W. (1973), *The History of the Post Office in British North America, 1639-1870*, Octagon Books, New York, NY.

Socknat, P. (1987), *Witness Against War: Pacifism in Canada*, 1900-1945, University of Toronto Press, Toronto.

Sotiron, M. (1992), "Concentration and collusion in the Canadian Newspaper Industry, 1895-1920", *Journalism History*, Vol. 18, pp. 26-32.

Splichal, S. (2002), "The principle of publicity, public use of reason and social control", *Media, Culture & Society*, Vol. 24, pp. 5-26.

Starr, P. (2004), *The Creation of the Media: Political Origins of Modern Communications*, Basic Books, New York, NY.

Syvertsen, T. (1999), "The many uses of the 'public service' concept", *Nordicom Review*, Vol. 20 No. 1, pp. 5-12.

Swyripa, F. and Thompson, J.H. (Eds) (1983), *Loyalties in Conflict: Ukrainians in Canada During the Great War*, Canadian Institute of Ukrainian Studies, University of Alberta, Edmonton.

Tester, J. (Ed.) (1986), *Sport Pioneers: A History of the Finnish-Canadian Amateur Sports Federation, 1906-1986*, Alerts AC Historical Committee, Sudbury.

Weinrich, P. (1982), *Social Protests from the Left in Canada*, 1870-1970 (a bibliography), University of Toronto Press, Toronto.

Winseck, D. (1998), *Reconvergence: A Political Economy of Telecommunications in Canada*, Hampton Press, Cresskill.

Wright, R. and Endres, R. (1976), *Eight Men Speak and other Plays from the Canadian Workers' Theatre*, New Hogtown Press, Toronto.

Young, W.D. (1969), *Anatomy of a Party: The National CCF 1932-61*, University of Toronto Press, Toronto.

10

Media in the New Political Order

Dorji Wangchuk

The article looks at the development of the modern mass media in Bhutan and the role it has played in the overall modernization process and what is expected from it in the future. It also attempts to engage with issues of press freedom, need for own media model, and the role of public service and the independent press in the changing political scenario. Bhutan is undergoing fundamental changes in politics, economy, social fabric, and every other aspect as a nation. In the new political environment mass media will play a vital role in sustaining the democracy. The special part of the Bhutan story is that the path to democracy has been forged by none other than the Monarch himself. The author feels that the success of the new path will depend a lot on how the media is managed and practiced in the country.

Premise

Bhutan is undergoing fundamental changes in politics, economy, social fabric and every other aspect as a nation. This is a defining moment for a country that has seen a peaceful idyllic existence for over a century. Whatever decisions are made, changes proposed, and conclusions drawn will have long-term implications on the country both as a 'State' and as a 'Nation'.

In the new political environment mass media will play a vital role in sustaining the democracy. In fact the success of the new path, so laboriously and single-handedly forged by His Majesty, will in large part depend on how the media is managed and practiced in the country. The *draft* Constitution guarantees the freedom of speech, press and expression in 'letters'.[1] Will these be translated into 'spirit' by the government that would have to regulate these rights and by citizens that would have to exercise these rights?

This paper looks at the development of the modern mass media in Bhutan and the role that it has played in the overall modernisation process. It attempts to answer the questions pertaining to issues such as press freedom in Bhutanese context, the need for a Bhutanese media model, and the role of the public service and the independent press in the changing political scenario. To simplify the argument presented in this paper, mass media shall mean print, radio, and television.

Background

To understand the growth of media and its role within the Bhutanese context, one has to appreciate the overall overarching development philosophy. This understanding is vital and it averts any prejudiced assessment or simplistic conclusion often drawn by Bhutan-watch groups and so-called upholders of press freedom in the world.

Bhutan is a tiny kingdom in the Eastern Himalayas still not widely known to the rest of the world. This is because the country remained in a self-imposed isolation until the first half of the twentieth century. The total superficial area of 38,394[2] square kilometres is sandwiched between India – to the south and China – to the north. Within these borders, the country rises into the higher Himalayas like a giant stairway, dramatically climbing up from the lush green tropical forests to some of the highest mountains in the world. The virtually untouched forest that covers 64.5 percent of the country is home to a large number of flora and fauna making Bhutan one of the world's hotspots in biodiversity.[2]

Although Bhutan is a comparatively small country in size, it has many diverse language groups among its small population. A total of 18 languages and numerous dialects are spoken among a population of 634,972.[3] Having never been colonised, the country developed a distinct culture and tradition over the millennia. Three main ethnic groups – Ngalong, Sharchop, and Nepali, and several other minorities are dispersed across a mountainous and difficult territory. Communication is still undeveloped, and except for a small group of population comprising government officials and business community, much of the Bhutanese people confine themselves within their farms in rural areas.

Until the sixties, Bhutan remained an isolated country, a forbidden kingdom. Only 13 Western expeditions had entered the country beginning with two Portuguese Jesuit missionaries – Cacella and Cabral in 1642.[4] This isolationist policy was to change forever with the enthronement of the third king of the Wangchuck dynasty – King Jigme Dorji Wangchuck, in 1952. The King recognised that if Bhutan were to survive as a nation, it had to modernise its economy and open its door to the outside world. Hence he initiated an intense political, social and economic reform starting with the institution of the National Assembly in 1953 as the parliament.[5]

In 1961, the first five-year development plan was launched with the focus on roads and social infrastructure, such as hospitals and schools.[6] In 1965, the Royal Advisory Council was instituted as a consultative body to advise the king and government and to supervise the implementation of programs and policies laid down by the national assembly.[7] Three years later in 1968, the Bank of Bhutan was created to regulate the economy and monetary policies.[8] In the same year, the Royal Court of Justice was established separating the judiciary from the executive arm of the government. In 1971, Bhutan was admitted to the United Nations as an independent and sovereign nation. The present King, His Majesty Jigme Singye Wangchuck, who succeeded to the throne in 1972 continued this process of modernisation and gave continuity to the progressive policy of the third King. Forty years of planned development have remarkably improved the living standard. The GDP per-capita now stands at US$1,321 – one of the highest in the South Asia.[9]

While the story of a nation's modernisation process is nothing extraordinary, what singles out Bhutan is the balance that this country has achieved between modernisation and cultural preservation, and between economic development and environmental conservation. In short, Bhutan has drawn on the global development experience and followed a unique development path carefully adopting what is good and not necessarily accepting everything coming from the West.

Development of Bhutanese Media

The development of media has followed the same overall development policy of slow, balanced, and calculated growth. Mass media in Bhutan until recently was comprised of *Kuensel,*[10] the national newspaper; BBS (Bhutan Broadcasting Service), the public service radio; TV; Internet; and cinema. This is not surprising as the country itself embarked on the modernization process only four decades ago.

When the modern economic development started in 1961, priority for development was on creation of basic physical infrastructure, such as roads and power stations, and social infrastructure, such as schools and hospitals. In such a situation, with decision-making concentrated in the capital, it was appropriate and adequate to have only the *Kuensel*, an official bulletin catering mainly to the officialdom. In fact, Kuensel did not start as a newspaper. It was more a development newsletter carrying short write-ups on important decisions and events revolving around the capital.

Similarly, radio was first broadcast in 1973 as a weekly service for the Thimphu area. It was initiated by an amateur radio operator and a group of volunteers of the erstwhile National Youth Association of Bhutan (NYAB). In fact the station was known as Radio NYAB. With the bureaucracy getting bigger and development activities increasing year-by-year, there was a need for wider coverage.

Radio NYAB became a full-fledged public service in 1979 after the station was brought under the erstwhile Department of Information & Broadcasting.

The Royal Government, realising the potential of radio to disseminate information, brought Radio NYAB under the wings of the Ministry of Communications. Further support from the government and external aid agencies led to the establishment of the Bhutan Broadcasting Service in June 1986.

As the curtain of the twentieth century drew to a close, Bhutan launched the broadcast television on June 2, 1999 and liberalised the media with foreign television stations beaming into the country from space. The day before, Bhutan was connected to the worldwide web (WWW) and cyberspace.

Finally in January 2005, the first two independent newspapers were licensed under private ownership, marking a new era in the Bhutanese media. While this was a surprise for many who never believed that Bhutan would accept the Western notion of a free press, for Bhutan connoisseurs and operators in the Bhutanese media, this development was seen as a natural progression of the media in the country. The seed for an independent press, in fact, was sown in 1992 when, by a Royal Decree, the two media organisations, BBS and Kuensel, were delinked from the government apparatus. The following is an excerpt of the Royal Decree:

> ....Today, as the kingdom enters the age of communications, its priorities are geared to meet the needs and demands of the times. The kingdom has seen a dramatic increase in the literacy rate of the population as a result of the special attention given by the Royal Government to the education sector. As technological advancement brings the international community closer together, it has also established the infrastructure to modernize and strengthen communications and information links with the rest of the world.
>
> It is the policy of the Royal Government, therefore, to facilitate and encourage the professional growth of the Bhutanese media, which must play an important and responsible role in all areas of development. Such role is especially relevant to the national policy of decentralization, which aims to involve all sections of the Bhutanese society in the socio-economic and political development of the Kingdom.
>
> The national newspaper, Kuensel, and the Bhutan Broadcasting Service will therefore be delinked from the Ministry of Communications to give

them the flexibility to grow in professionalism and to enable them to be more effective in fulfilling their important responsibility to society. From the fifth day of the eighth Bhutanese month (October 1, 1992) the national newspaper, Kuensel, and the Bhutan Broadcasting Service will be established as two autonomous corporations. The Kuensel and BBS Corporations will be governed by an editorial board comprising of representatives of the government, media professionals, scholars, and eminent citizens.

His Majesty Jigme Singye Wangchuck, King of Bhutan.

The decree clearly specified the mandate and professional role of the Bhutanese media, aside from implying fresh directions and responsibility.[11] It is often referred to as the turning point in the history of media development in Bhutan.

It can, therefore, be concluded that the growth of media has been in consonance with the socio-economic development of the country. It reflected the changes taking place in the social, political, and economic evolution of the country.

Freedom of Press – Absolute or Relative

One of the most recurrent questions a Bhutanese pressman hears is *how free is the Bhutanese media?* There is no straightforward answer to this simple enquiry, for freedom of press is not an absolute concept but a relative term. Nowhere in the world, not even in the greatest democracies such as the US, is there anything called 'absolute' press freedom. The pro-American views adopted by American media during the last war in Afghanistan and the ongoing occupation of Iraq are latest examples of how nations, who preach the idea of free press, actually carry out such practices in reality. On the other hand, the American Constitution does not mention press freedom as fundamental rights *per se*. Rather, it is only mentioned as an off-shoot of freedom of speech guaranteed by the First Amendment passed by Congress in 1791. Across the Atlantic, Article 10 of the European Convention even suggests 'permissible' modification of the press freedom to protect the security of a nation, public health and moral, and to oppose racism and violence.[12] Hence, press freedom in an absolute sense is an ideal and like any ideal it remains enshrined somewhere distant from reality.

Having accepted that freedom is actually *relative*, one can affirm that Bhutanese pressmen have always enjoyed *relative* press freedom. It has never been a state policy to stop the growth of the media. If situations, circumstances and conditions have proved otherwise, it is because certain bureaucrats and individuals equated themselves to the 'State' or to the 'Government'. And even when personal or institutional weaknesses were revealed or shortcomings exposed, senior government officials often linked the action of the press as an attack to the "Tsa wa sum" (King, country, and the people). Other times, bureaucrats maintained a defensive stand against the media. The most common occurrences were over-zealous subordinates who would make the press a scapegoat to win favours from the rich or the powerful.

The draft Constitution of Bhutan explicitly guarantees the freedom of speech, press, and expression. This is a big commitment rarely seen in other countries of the world. But as the country gets closer to adopting this Constitution, there is a growing misconception that some sort of *grand* free-for-all situation is on the horizon. But freedom entails sense of responsibility. In fact a *great* sense of responsibility, both for operators as well as for ordinary citizens. Freedom of press does not mean freedom to write anything one likes. Freedom of speech does not mean freedom to insult or defame somebody. There are individual rights and privacy to be respected and social well being of the community to be taken care of. Unless the media gives more weight to such social norms, it will become far from a credible source of information working for the social good.

Nor can an individual media-person use the press and people around him or her to gather solidarity around his or her beliefs. Freedom of speech is an *individual* freedom while freedom of press is that of an *institution*. While journalists and producers may exercise their freedom of speech as individuals, they may not use the press as platforms to reach thousands of Bhutanese. This is as unethical as barring the freedom itself.

Factors Limiting the Press Freedom and Responsibility of Free Press

Having practiced and having to practice the press freedom what are then the variables or factors that determine, or limit, the press freedom? What does it really mean by the term a *responsible* press?

Media in different countries plays different roles. These roles are based on historical experiences, racial mixtures, cultural settings, political systems and levels of human development. The combination of these factors in varying degrees is what defines the media in a country. Every country therefore works out a media model that suits itself the best. There is no universal standard or yardstick, although quite often, Western nations have tried, and continue to insist on the Western model as the universal media model.

Historical Background

All over the globe, there has been a basic consideration in the way the concepts of press freedom historically shaped themselves. In the UK, the distinguishing stamp on the press freedom is undoubtedly the Official Secret Act. In India, the growth of a vibrant anti-colonial nationalist press before the independence was the watermark of the press that subsequently developed as a powerful element of freedom and democracy. Singapore always played by the motto of less-freedom-and-more-prosperity and went on to achieve the material wealth comparable with any Western nation. The Philippines is perhaps a good model of how a press should *not* be, with a grand free-for-all situation where the infamous *envelope journalism* has its roots and is still a widespread practice today.

In all above cases it is evident that every country has developed the media in relation to the historical experiences that the country has gone through. Modern Bhutanese media is an off-shoot of the modern development process initiated in 1961. Both the press and the broadcast media focused on development communications. In fact, the mission statement of BBS is "to act as a bridge between the people and the government and contribute to the socio-economic development of the country".[13] Much of the programming on BBS radio reflects this statement in that a large chunk is dedicated to development programmes such as improved farming methods, better livestock management, non-formal education, etc. The historical role of the BBS was therefore purely developmental, whereby the media would assist the government in the overall effort of nation building.

Ethnic Consideration

Although a small kingdom, Bhutan is a very diverse country in terms of racial mixtures and ethnic composition. The long isolation with the outside world and within the districts and regions has sown the seeds for intense regionalist feelings. And though planned economic development has connected every district in the country, encouraging massive movement of people and goods from one region to another, it will still take some more generations for Bhutanese to think as a nation. Hence the notion that "the rules of news judgment call for ignoring story implication"[14] would be disastrous. In simple terms, if a man rapes a woman, the press cannot report that the perpetrator is a *ngalop* (western Bhutanese) and the victim is a *sharchop* (eastern Bhutanese) or vice versa. Little does it matter that these *are* the facts. Such disregard for ethnic sensitivity could inflame the delicate balance between different ethnic groups in the country. The overall effect on journalism, one could argue, is that there is a loss of news objectivity. However, in exchange for social harmony, reporters should often compromise their professionalism and ethics. In neighbouring India, in 1992, it is believed that the demolition of the Babri Mosque shown *live* on BBC TV via satellite had spurred communal violence all over India. The TV channel should have considered the social implication of showing jubilant religious fanatics at work. Similarly, multi-ethnic countries such as Malaysia, Singapore, Indonesia and even UK have adopted this editorial policy.

Cultural Competence

Cultural competence is defined as a set of behaviours, attributes and policies enabling an agency or an individual to work in cross-cultural settings and situations. The rugged mountainous terrain of Bhutan has for thousands of years impeded the intra-regional communications and cultural exchange. This has led to the evolution of distinct culture and tradition between regions. Cultural conservation is considered one of the four pillars of the GNH (gross national happiness). Hence, media persons should exercise cultural competence in their line of duty. If local traditions call for certain behaviours and ethics, which reporters may find unusual or comical, they should not criticize or mock at the ways things happen.

In Bhutan, culture is almost synonymous with religion and hence any disdain on the culture could be viewed as direct blasphemy or act of profanity. In a country where religious sentiments still run high, such acts would entail problems within communities and groups.

A story goes that in a village in Africa, a documentary screening session ended up in a brawl because the documentary contained a scene of a chicken crossing the screen. Apparently this act was inauspicious and the owner of the chicken (on screen) had to be identified and reprimanded for not taking a good care of the chicken. Only after that could the evening resume.

Political System

A political system and its evolution play an important role in shaping the media in a country. The political history of America has enabled the development of a press which unfortunately cannot be transplanted in Bhutan which has been a medieval-state until the nineteen sixties. Democratic societies have been in the forefront in promoting press freedom. This is not to say that other forms of governance have not encouraged a free press. Monarchies such as Japan, Thailand, and even Italy (before World War II) have a vibrant press and journalism.

In Bhutan, the political system has definitely shaped the modern media. A significant deviation from the Western norm is a strong sense of national loyalty. The traditional *zhung-dang-mitse-damtsi* (government-people relation) extended to media-persons. This is mainly because Bhutan has been blessed with a leadership whose concern for the welfare of the people has never been in doubt. Hence, the media, with rare exception, ended up adopting the government's position on almost everything. Patriotism or national loyalty may be a *passé* in the west. In Bhutan, it is still very strong. This practice gave the view that the media was under the strict control of the government. In reality, the common editorial policy practiced by Bhutanese media has been that of forging a sense of national identity and sense of nation-hood under the figure head of the monarchy. This is for obvious reasons. A country sandwiched between two giants can only survive through a strong sense of national unity.

Freedom of Expression and Censorship

Freedom of expression is termed as a means of seeking, receiving, and imparting information or ideas regardless of the medium used. It goes beyond the freedom of speech into non-verbal form of communication such as art, films, pictures, songs, dances, way of dressing, looks, etc.

If freedom of expression is explicitly guaranteed by the constitution, then the existing government mechanisms to control or censor, such as the national film and TV review board, become unconstitutional. This board has been set up to censor and certify Bhutanese films for public consumption, which is sensible in light of social, political and cultural implications that a film might possibly have, not to mention the breach in state security and safety. But as people become self-centred and greedy, some unpleasant events might overrun the otherwise good work of the board. It may be necessary therefore to review the mandate, functions, and responsibility of such boards and committees taking into consideration the freedom of expression on one side and responsibility on the other.

Then there is the restriction on civil servants to sing, act in films, write articles and columns, and talk to the press. On one hand freedom of speech and expression are granted and on the other, age-old methods still seem to prevail in Bhutan. Democracy and free press are concepts that unfortunately come as a package. One cannot welcome Democracy and shut the door to free press. There cannot be a vibrant democracy without a dynamic press.

Threats to Freedom

When one refers to threat to press freedom, one is immediately inclined to think of regulators, legislators, dictators, and autocrats who *either* don't believe in free press or fear them. The fact is that there can be two kinds of threats – threats from *external restrictions* and threats from *within.*

External Restrictions

Threats from external restrictions include censorship, legislation, government regulations, and other measures and practices that restrict the job of pressmen. In an editorial for *Bhutan Times*, Editor Tashi Phuntsho writes: "Media may be granted freedom but when there is censorship at the source of events, it defeats the purpose. The door is increasingly shut to us." Despite the rapid pace of progress and the overall achievement in socio-economic spheres, the sad reality is that restrictions exist. Not so much as state policies, but rather as personal considerations or individual decisions. Perhaps it is owing to the feudal past, or may be it is because of the Bhutanese modesty and humility at work. Whatever the reason, people still prefer to operate in secrecy, within their little 'pond', totally apprehensive of any external presence. Any intrusion or attempt to intrude is met with disapproving faces and defensive actions. Defensiveness reflects fear, the fear of discovered dishonesty, revealed complicity or, at best, lack of self-confidence. Such an attitude neither augurs well for the establishment nor for the press itself. For it undermines the national policy of efficiency, accountability, and transparency. Not to mention the breach in Article 7.5 of the Constitution that guarantees the citizens right to information. How much these rights are respected by those in power will remain to be seen.

Internal Threats

Threats from within are internal (individual or institutional) threats. These are as dangerous as external threats. In case of Bhutan, they are even more. They stem from self-censorship, irresponsibility, inaccuracy, and lack of professionalism by media personnel, as well as outright corruption by reporters and editors for personal gain. Again the fault does not lie entirely with the journalist. Sometimes the reason could be simple: low salary and poor working conditions. Unless a journalist enjoys a good pay and a decent living standard, he or she would fall prey to corruption and envelope-journalism.

Institutional threats are caused by childish delight of owners and chief executives masquerading as editors and journalists. Managers, who have no background in media, do not recognise media-persons as professionals and moreover tend to 'advise' the subordinates. Internal threats degrade the credibility, responsibility, and journalistic ethics of the press.

Consequences of Threats

Threats, whether internal or external, do achieve one common goal – they weaken the press. Such a scenario will be disastrous in the wake of the political reforms in the country. The necessary condition for a vibrant democracy is a dynamic and responsible press. A feeble or a muzzled press would therefore undermine the whole democratic experiment. For, it is only through the media that people can express their wishes freely thereby holding the authorities accountable to the populace and redirecting their plans and priorities. However, it is a well-known fact, though generally not accepted, that Bhutanese at all levels are allergic to criticisms no matter how well-intended or how best they are worded. Even in the lower level of bureaucracy, to submit even a constructive criticism to an individual would be to invite a fierce defensive, and sometimes offensive, stance by the entire institution. Worse still, the issue is given higher importance attracting counter-suits and allegations of being judgmental, biased, and detrimental to the image of the State.

One of the flaws of democracy is that there could be a leader who is incapable, inept, and inefficient, or a combination of all three. Such a leader could nevertheless equate himself to the State, and any attempt to uncover his wrongdoings or shortcomings could be likened to an attack against the State. Any criticism to his plans and policies could be taken as an assault to the social harmony of the nation.

In India, the government-press relation is still governed by Mahatma Gandhi's enlightened statement that "the national cause will never suffer by honest criticism of national institution and national policies". This far-reaching and visionary dictum explains perhaps the very high quality of journalism standards in India – some comparable to the best in the world.

As new leadership take the helm of governance in Bhutan, would they accept positive comments and constructive criticisms? Or will they also retaliate with vague reasons and restrictive regulations in the name of national security, identity and harmony and good relations with friendly countries?

Role of Media in a Changing Political Scenario

Bhutan is going through fundamental changes. Unlike other countries that greet the changes with political turmoil and civil unrest, Bhutan is blessed with a leadership that is managing the changes as a peaceful evolution rather than as a violent transition. However, for such peaceful means to fully succeed, media –

both public service and independent – must play a crucial role. They must inform and shape public opinion. They must educate the masses on the changes, challenges, choices, and eventual benefits. Only then can people make informed choices and play a significant role by actively participating in political changes.

Role of Public Service Media

One of the sacred roles of the public service media is to offer citizens universal, equal, and unimpeded access to information. Public service media also has the societal and cultural obligation to help bind the nation together by promoting social equity (that rich and poor alike should have the same opportunities to receive programs).

The public service media has in large part operated as an extension of the government within the overall context of nation-building. However, employees of the two public service media have been given the step-motherly treatment. Neither do the employees get the benefits rendered to the civil servant nor the financial incentives enjoyed by other corporate workers. In this period when the wisdom of having public enterprises is being questioned, publicly owned media cannot be taken for granted, and their objectives and obligations are no longer self-evident. Therefore, there is a need to redefine the roles, mandate, and funding mechanisms for the public service media.

There is no question of whether Bhutan needs the public service media or not. It is clear that as independent media gets their financing from corporate entities (which will have political inclinations), the role of the public service as a credible source of balanced reports, unbiased analysis, and impartial programming is vital for the success of a democratic society. This is again not to question the professionalism of the independent press. The Media Act in fact bars the editorial interventions of owners and CEOs. But how much this is applied and monitored is another issue.

If an appropriate funding mechanism is not worked out for the public service media, what could also happen is that instead of reaching out to the districts, the public service media could be bogged down competing for a share of audience, improving the ratings, and capturing the urban market where money flows. This will leave the un-economical areas like rural Bhutan unreported in the mainstream media.

Public Service Radio

Few years back, a government minister was visiting the remote valley of Merak Sakten in the higher Himalayas, inhabited by a semi-nomadic group, known among others for the foul smell that radiates from their body and dress. Every morning from the window of the guesthouse where our minister was hosted, he would see an old man defying the early morning chill to go and wash in the cold icy waters of the Himalayas. On enquiring the man, our minister was told, "I am having my regular bath". Amused, the minister carried on, "But don't you feel the cold?" "Well I was told I should take regular bath if I am to stay healthy," the man replied. More amused, our minister asked, "And who told you that?" "I heard it on the radio," came the reply. This short story portrays the power of the radio and the presence of this medium in the daily lives of rural Bhutan, comprising about 70 percent of the country's total population.

Radio is by far the most important media for the Bhutanese people. The very mountainous terrain, deep gorges, fast flowing rivers, and dense jungles make radio the effective tool for disseminating information. In some remote isolated communities, especially among semi-nomadic pastoral groups of Laya, Lingshi, Lunana, and Merak Sakten, radio is the only source of entertainment, information, and education.

Bhutan is still very much an agrarian society with 70 percent of Bhutanese still living in the rural area[15] on subsistence farming. It is here among the simple and often illiterate farmers that radio has the widest audience. Media Impact Study 2006 commissioned by the Ministry of Information shows that there are around 83,000 radio receivers in the country with a total listening population of 400,000,[16] which is equivalent to 88.6 percent[17] of the total population. The study also shows that in terms of people's specific pBibliography, it is radio, closely followed by television. About 45.93 percent of the respondents preferred the radio while 45.72 percent prefer TV.

Public Service TV

> I would like to remind our youth that the television and the Internet provide a whole range of possibilities which can be both beneficial as well as negative for the individual and the society. I trust that you will exercise your good sense and judgment in using the Internet and television.
>
> – King Jigme Singye Wangchuck, 2 June 1999

Broadcast television came to Bhutan in 1999. From one-hour transmissions confined to the capital city of Thimphu the service has been extended nation-wide with a daily programming of five hours. While the public service radio models itself as a developmental radio, television has successfully established itself as a public forum for discussions on issues facing the society. Hence, in light of the fundamental political changes, TV more than radio, has the potential for providing public space for discussion on issues facing the society. Such debates are vital in shaping public opinion, which is but a crystallization of the freely expressed wishes of the people. Public opinion will have bearing on the governance of the country, thereby fulfilling the ideals of democracy.

What is not very clear is the capacity of the present public service TV to organize evocative public debates on meaningful issues confronting the society. The broadcast media has been managed by civil servants, of different managerial capacities, some good and some who left much to be desired. The one common result was the limitation of the journalistic and professional growth. Although by a Royal Decree of 1992, BBS was to function as an autonomous corporation, for all practical matters, it had to "abide" by some unwritten code of management. This was often some casual remarks here, some indiscriminate views there, passed by some prominent people. The management would often put producers, reporters and editors at the receiving end of unpleasant "briefings". The net result has been a flourishing practice of self-censorship where reporters and editors would censor out facts even before any reaction has been received.

Then there is the unique Bhutanese journalism which one could term as 'speech' journalism where the prime time news is dominated by speeches, workshops, and inaugurations by senior government officials. Editors often wait for press handouts and reporters are often "invited" to, and attend, the numerous workshops and conferences. This has left the major chunk of the population either un-reported or under-reported.

Although the newest of the three traditional media, TV, has caught on to the audience who prefer watching TV more than reading paper or listening to radio. Besides, television, being the most powerful medium, has the social responsibility to conduct and encourage TV debates on various issues affecting the nation. It can bring the nation together through socially and culturally diverse programming and content.

Public Service Print

Kuensel (meaning clarity) was started in 1967 as an official bulletin. It was brought to the present tabloid format in 1986. From 500 copies, Kuensel now sells over 15,000 (Saturday issue) and 12,000 (Wednesday issue) copies with an estimated readership of 200,000 *(Source: Kuensel).* Kuensel is increasingly opening up and becoming a credible source of news. However, many still believe that Kuensel is government-controlled. While the broadcast media caters to the rural population, Kuensel has the potential to stir public debate, shape the opinion, and contribute to the overall political discourse—mainly for the educated elite. In fact it has grown to be a powerful force of democracy having initiated online debates and editorials that touch on issues of social and national importance.

Endowment Fund

As Bhutan moves unenthusiastically towards 2008 when democracy and party politics will take hold, the role of the media remains crucial to the success of the political reforms. Once the transition to 2008 has been made, the position of the public service media, especially BBS, will remain a dilemma. BBS receives much of its funding as a subsidy from the government. This funding mechanism could prove to be "tricky" as the government in power could use the annual subsidy to impose their terms and conditions. What could happen is that the public service media, that is supposed to stay out of partisan politics, will have to foster closer ties with political decision-makers to keep the show going. One cannot argue that *sin qua;* both BBS and Kuensel were often considered as an extension of the "civil service", which was synonymous for government, state or the nation. In the new political order, the single sacrosanct *Zhung* (government) will be replaced by many state entities—the political debates dominated by two opposing factions, the ruling and the opposition parties.

Hence, the public service media cannot, and should not, represent the ruling government if they are to maintain public credibility and faith. Hence, the operation of the public service media should be met through an "endowment fund" to be granted to the public service print, radio, and TV. This fund should not be at the discretion of any government. Rather it should come with an Act passed by the National Assembly that would require the government to release the money with no conditions attached.

Challenges – Globalisation

One of the challenges for the Bhutanese media is to contain the impact of global media. Globalisation has not spared even this Lost Horizon. *Coca Cola* is already operational with its first plant in the kingdom. *Pepsi* has been around for quite sometime now. *Nokia* has started connecting the Bhutanese people while the Airbus ferries fresh *sushis* and *Hagen Daz* ice cream under the Druk Air banner. Fortunately, with the recent nation-wide ban on the sale of tobacco products, Bhutan is not a *Marlboro country*.

Yet, more than these commodities, it is the direct-to-home satellites that may have an irreversible impact on the age-old culture and tradition that have survived till the dawn of this millennium. Today, nothing less than 45 foreign channels are available in every urban home in Bhutan—with CNN International being the first to tell us what we should know and *Fashion TV* showing us how our girls should look.

The effects of global television are very visible. Cricket, which was virtually unknown before the advent of cable television, is today the fastest growing sport among our youngsters. Cricket may perhaps be the brighter side of the story depending on whether or not one loves this sport. What is more alarming for any sensitive observer is the fact that global television is connected with the ideology of global capitalism, a force intent on distraction, cultural assimilation, and consumer creation. Traditionally, the Bhutanese, as pious Buddhists, cultivate from an early age a slow and subtle appreciation for values of life and simplicity. Commercial television promotes just the opposite – individualism and unscrupulous consumerism and puts life on the fast lane. It is not surprising therefore, that in the few years since the arrival of TV in Bhutan, private ownership of cars have grown from 7,438 in 1999 to 11,428 in 2003.[18]

The explosion of capitalism and the growth of the urban centres are fuelling another problem—the rural-urban migration. Studies have shown that this migration is taking place at an alarming rate of 10 percent per annum[19]. On the other hand, the average age of the general population is going down and youngsters are more inclined towards foreign media and commodities. In either of the above cases, radio will not have any listeners a few years down the line.

Finally, the presence of international media in even the remotest villages is now inevitable. New technologies continue to bring civilisations closer and yet at the same time threaten to tear the world apart. Under such a scenario, decision-makers, media executives, and professionals should have a better understanding of national policies and local priorities. Eventually there is the need to develop a strong sense of local identity of the media to suit local needs. This localisation of programme content is what will give the ownership and sense of identity to the listeners. Oddly, in the age of globalisation, the secret of survival is staying local. To quote, more or less, one Indian media executive, it does not matter to an ordinary Indian farmer, whether it rains or shines in New York or London. What he needs to know is whether there would be enough rain before the rice plantation season. And this information is something only a local media can give.

Quo Vadis – From There to Here to Where?

From development journalism that the Bhutanese media has always been, where does it go from here? What direction does it take in light of the fundamental changes in the country? There are three areas of recommendations:

Need to Develop a 'Bhutanese' Media Model

Media, as we have seen, does not have a universal standard that can be applied in every country. It varies from country to country and from region to region.

On one hand, there is the need for the media to reflect the Bhutanese culture and society. On the other, the influence of the media in a "new" Bhutan is so great that one cannot overlook the need to understand the media itself.

Hence, there is the need to develop a Bhutanese media model – considering the nation's history, culture, ethnic composition, level of human development, and the role the Bhutanese media has played thus far.

Re-define the Role of Public Service Media

There is also the need to redefine the role of the public service media. From development journalism there is the need to go further into shaping the public opinion on national issues, providing equitable coverage, enhancing the cause of nationhood, and watering the seeds of a democratic society. There is the need to go from just plain reporting to involve and encourage discussions and debates and carry the country forward.

Carryout Massive Media Literacy Programme

The absence of an independent media has created a *quasi*-divine status for the mass media which is synonymous with BBS and Kuensel. As commercial media comes into the market there is the need to educate the people on how to view media more critically, in essence to become media-literate. People need to understand that whatever comes from the media is not the absolute truth. Media literacy programmes should be carried out among all sections of the society – especially students.

Legislation—the New Dilemma

The job of the media has never been an easy one. Until now it had to understand the target audience and tailor-make any information that was disseminated. On different occasions, media is often accused of being on opposite sides by warring parties. In worst of cases it becomes the sacrificial lamb. The general expectation, again, was that with the adoption of the Constitution and media legislation, things would improve. In fact the opposite was expected and that exactly what has happened. The job of the pressmen has become even harder because the line that marks the borders between do's and don'ts will become hazy. And with no clear directives or professional maturity to decide what can be reported and what should be left out, journalists and editors are in a total dilemma.

Closing Words

Bhutan has always had the wisdom and political commitment to balance growth and happiness. As the doors were flung open to modernisation and winds of change blew across the Eastern Himalayas, Bhutan has not adopted everything coming from the West but has had the ingenuity to choose skilfully things that can best serve its interests. At times, Bhutan seems to have perfected the art of modifying Western concepts and culture to suit her own needs.

With the entry of global concepts like free press and democracy into the homes of every Bhutanese where evening dinner talks around the kitchen fireplace could be centred on multi-party politics, it may not be a surprise if Bhutan again skilfully responds by reconciling politics and press freedom with traditional "Bhutanese" values and ways of doing things. If the new mantra of the Bhutanese continues, it will be similar to a Bollywood classic *Shri 420* where Raj Kapoor sings: "my shoes are Japanese/these pants are British/the cap on my head is Russian/but my heart is Indian."

(Dorji Wangchuk is an electronic engineer turned documentary filmmaker who pioneered the introduction of TV in Bhutan. He is a columnist, broadcast engineer, TV host and media consultant; runs a private media firm, Chenzig Communications that provides films, documentaries and media services. He can be reached at dorjiwangchuck@yahoo.com).

Endnotes

1 Article 7.2 of the Constitution of the Kingdom of Bhutan.

2 Ninth Plan document, Planning Commission, Royal Government of Bhutan, 2002.

3 National Housing & Population Census, 2005.

4 Francoise Pommaret, Introduction to Bhutan, Odyssey publications.

5 The National Assembly is composed of 150 members. 100 representatives of the people elected to the post for three years tenure, 10 members of the clergy and thirty representatives of the government.

6 Karma Ura, "The Bhutanese development story", Kuensel, 23 January 2004.

7 Statistical Yearbook of Bhutan 2003, National Statistical Bureau, Royal Government of Bhutan, March 2004.

8 The function of the central bank would later be transferred to the Royal Monetary Authority created in 1982.

9 Bhutan Poverty Analysis Report, National Statistical Bureau, Royal Government of Bhutan, August 2004.

10 Kuensel newspaper was started in 1967 as an official bulletin of the Royal Government. It later became a full fledged newspaper in June 1986. In 1992, it became independent of the government by the Royal Decree of 1992. It is published bi-weekly, on Wednesdays and Saturdays.

11 Kuensel editorial, 19 February 2005.

12 Chua Lee Hoong, Press Freedom and Professional Standards in Asia, AMIC, Singapore.

13 BBS Mission Statement, Ninth Plan Document, 2002.

14 Sunanda Dutta Ray, Press Freedom and Professional Standards in Asia AMIC, Singapore.

15 Bhutan Poverty Analysis Report, National Statistical Bureau, Royal Government of Bhutan, August 2004.

16 BBS Audience Survey 2000, Danida/Roots Consultancy.

17 Media Impact Study 2003, Siok Sian Pek.

18 Statistical Yearbook of Bhutan 2003, National Statistical Bureau, Royal Government of Bhutan, March 2004.

19 Pem Gyeltshen, Rural Urban Migration, Asian Institute of Technology, Bangkok.

11

Media Use in Estonia

Trends and Patterns*

Peeter Vihalemm

The article gives an overview of general trends in media use in Estonia over the last 15 years, making some comparisons with Nordic countries. Since the beginning of postcommunist transformation in 1991, the media landscape in Estonia has faced substantial changes. A completely renewed media system has emerged, characterized by a diversity of channels, formats, and contents. Not only the media themselves, but also the patterns of media use among audiences, their habits and expectations, have gone through a process of radical change. Changes in the Estonian media landscape have some aspects in common with many other European countries, such as the impact of emerging new media and global TV; others are specific features of transition to a market economy and democratic political order. Besides discussing general trends, the article gives insights into some audience-related aspects of changes, more specifically age and ethnicity.

* The article is based on research supported by the Estonian Ministry of Education and Science (research theme 1774) and Estonian Science Foundation (grant 6526).

Introduction

Despite the strong pressure of the Soviet propaganda system, Estonian-language journalism maintained its role as a social integrator and played an important role in cultural resistance of Estonians to the totalitarian regime (see Høyer, Lauk & Vihalemm 1993; Vihalemm & Lauristin 1997). Looking back at the 1970s and 1980s, general media use in Estonia was among the most active in the Soviet Union: the amount of radio listening and press reading was comparable to the very high levels of the Nordic countries. The Estonian language press was popular among all sectors of the population. In the early 1980s an average Estonian regularly read 7 newspapers and magazines (Lauristin *et al* 1987: 88).

According to surveys of the sociological research group of Estonian Radio and Estonian Television (see Vihalemm 2001), the average TV viewing time per day was 1 hour 30 minutes in 1976 and 2 hours in 1983-1985; radio listening time was 3 hours and 3 hours 10 minutes respectively (Saar 1985; Paulson 1986).

During the period of glasnost, when the multi-party system did not yet exist and the underground centres were weak, the media was the main mechanism of mass mobilisation (see Lauristin & Vihalemm, 1993; Lauristin, 1998; Tapinas, 1998). In the first phase of postcommunist transition, characterised by the rise of the mass political movements (1987-1991), media in the three Baltic countries had played an active role in mobilisation and integration of people around national values (Hoyer, Lauk & Vihalemm 1993; Lauristin & Vihalemm 2002). Media use grew along with the audience's interest in politics, reaching a peak in 1989-1990. In 1990, according to a survey of the Department of Journalism at Tartu University, an average Estonian regularly read 12.5 newspapers and magazines. The 1989-1990 period was the peak of press circulation in all Estonian history. Three national dailies with circulations of 150,000-200,000 each, a cultural weekly with a circulation of 90,000, a women's magazine of 225,000, etc. were published for a market of less than one million Estonians. In three years, 1988-1990, the total number of periodicals increased 3.7 times and their total circulation doubled.

Use of electronic media increased as well, though to a smaller extent compared to print media. The average radio listening time in 1989 was 3 hours 20 minutes per day, TV viewing time 2 hours 40 minutes respectively (Paulson 1993). During the period of mass political movements, broadcasting was extremely important as a mechanism of public participation.

Baltic opposition politicians fully utilised the ability of broadcast media – with their direct online access to a mass audience – to mobilise people and to stimulate protest movements. For instance, the two-million-person demonstration "Baltic chain", organised on 23 August 1989, the 50th anniversary of the Molotov-Ribbentrop pact, was not only directly broadcast on all radio and TV channels in Estonia, Latvia and Lithuania, but it was also organised and managed with the assistance of the media.

After the restoration of Estonian independence in August 1991, a new political and economic environment brought major changes in the media system and in the character of media use.

During the second stage of transition in 1991-1994, liberalisation of the press was closely related to abolition of state ownership and subsidies for the print media. Most of the newspapers were privatised and hundreds of new periodicals established. At the same time, a rapid generational turnover of journalists occurred (see Lauk, 1996, 1997). The new generation of journalists did not share the experiences and role models of their older colleagues, who took for granted an important political role for journalists in society. The new journalists quickly accepted an Anglo-Saxon model of news journalism and accepted marketisation of journalism as a natural process. The products of journalistic activities were increasingly evaluated according to their "sale value" as profitable goods, not as socially and culturally valuable texts. Competition for the attention of the audience has brought about changes in the content and functions of the media. Information and entertainment have intertwined, superseding analysis, enlightenment, and social integration (Vihalemm, Lauk & Lauristin 1997; Lauristin & Vihalemm 2002; Lauk & Harro 2003).

Increasing living costs, including a rise in the prices of newspapers and magazines (in the interval 1991-1996 they rose about three times more than the prices of other goods and services) led to a dramatic decrease in circulation and subscription to Estonian press publications. The pattern of media usage among Estonians also changed: reading newspapers became a more elite habit; many people were no longer able to subscribe even to one newspaper.

With the ongoing privatisation of the newspaper media, new magazines and private radio and TV channels were also launched. The result was a growing diversification and fragmentation of the media in the 1990s: instead of a few channels followed by a majority of the people, there was a growing number of channels followed by specific, smaller audiences.

Along with the establishment of new commercial radio stations from 1991 and commercial TV stations from 1993 onwards, the time spent on electronic media increased. At the same time, consumption of the printed press decreased. In 1995, compared to 1990, an average Estonian was reading regularly two times fewer newspapers and magazines (6.1); whereas the average radio listening time per day had grown to 4 hours and 12 minutes, TV viewing time increased to 3 hours 28 minutes (Lauristin & Vihalemm 1998: 33).

The Recent Picture: Stabilisation on New Levels

Since 1995 newspaper reading has stabilised, with a tendency toward a slight decrease. During the second half of the 1990s, when the first shock of radical reforms was over and the living standard of Estonian population started to rise, a large number of new magazines was launched. The number of magazines and other periodicals increased seven times during the 1990s. The growth in magazine reading was much more modest but still remarkable. Trends in radio listening and TV viewing moved in opposite directions – the average radio listening time decreased in the late 1990s, while TV viewing increased (Lauristin & Vihalemm 1998: 33).

Comparing the levels of Estonians' media use in 1999 with the level of 1984, we can see a decrease in newspaper reading, maintenance of the same level in magazine reading, and a remarkable increase in radio listing and especially in TV viewing – see Table 1.

Table 2 characterises the level of media use in 2004 in comparison with 2000. Table 3 presents general indicators of media use in the years 2000-2004 (in November of the respective year).

Table 1: Trends in Estonians' Media Use, 1984-1999 (1984=100)

	1984	1990	1994	1997	1999
Average number of newspapers regularly read	100	152	110	95	80
Average number of magazines and other periodicals regularly read	100	135	62	92	105
Average TV viewing time per day	100	128	146	180	185
Average radio listening time per day	100	125	155	132	130

Sources: Research Department of Estonian Radio, Department of Journalism at Tartu University, TNS Emor (BMF Gallup Media).

Table 2: Recent Trends of Media Use in Estonia 2000-2004 (2000=100)

	2000	2001	2002	2003	2004
Average number of newspapers regularly read	100	99	94	93	87
Average number of periodicals regularly read	100	102	92	90	75
Average TV viewing time per day	100	106	115	96*	97*
Average radio listening time per day	100	100	100	140*	135*
Share of Internet users	100	115	154	165	168

* Change in data collection methodology since January 2003 – TV meters introduced instead of viewers' diaries, and more precise determination of radio listening.

Source: TNS Emor.

Radio listening stabilised during the years 2000-2002 at a level of 3 hours 29 minutes, measured in autumn of the each respective year. The average TV viewing time has continually increased, with an average of 4 hours 30 minutes for the year 2002. In international comparison Estonia reached the level of the Top 5 television viewing countries in Europe and in the world (Hasebrink & Herzog 2004: 147).

Table 3: Aggregated Indicators of Media Use in Estonia, 2000-2004

	2000	2001	2002	2003	2004
Newspaper reading					
General reading (share of readers, %[1])	94.5	93.8	95.3	92.0	90.8
Regular readers (share of readers, %[2])	79.0	75.9	78.1	74.5	70.5
Average number of newspapers generally read	4.05	3.69	3.86	3.71	3.35
Average number of newspapers regularly read	2.11	2.08	1.98	1.97	1.83
Reading of magazines					
General reading (share of readers, %[3])	86.3	85.9	85.3	85.3	80,7
Regular readers (share of readers, %[4])	72.3	73.1	71.3	69.7	63.8
Average number of magazines generally read	5.57	5.47	4.96	4.65	3.99
Average number of magazines regularly read	2.55	2.59	2.35	2.30	1.92
Radio: average listening time per day (h: min)	3:29	3:29	3:29	4:52*	4:41*
Television: viewing time per day (h: min)	4:14	4:28	4:50	4:04*	4:06*
Internet: have used during last six months (%)	28.2	32.5	43.5	46.6	47.4**

1 Have read at least one of the last six issues of any newspaper

2 Have read at least four of the last six issues of any newspaper

3 Have read at least one of the last six issues of any magazine or other periodical

4 Have read at least four of the last six issues of any magazine or other periodical

* Change in data collection methodology since January 2003 – TV meters introduced instead of viewers' diaries, more precise determination of radio listening.

** These data contradict TNS Emor Internet usage survey data from spring 2004 when the ratio of Internet users among population aged 6-74 was 52% – Emor 2004.

Source: TNS Emor Ltd.

It is important to mention that changes in TV viewing and radio listening figures in 2003 and 2004 compared to previous years reflect changes in methodology, not in actual media use.[1] In early 2003 the leading Estonian opinion and market research company TNS Emor, which has been carrying out audience monitoring since 1993, introduced TV meters (electronic devices connected to TV sets) to replace TV viewing diaries. Changes were also made in sample composition: instead of population aged 12-74, all people older than 4 years were included in the survey. Because of these changes in data collection methodology, it is important to point out that the data in the Table 1, reflecting TV viewing and radio listening in 2003 and 2004, are not exactly comparable with the data from 2000-2002.

The Internet arrived in Estonia relatively early, in June 1992. Since 1995 Internet access and usage have increased rapidly (see Herron 1999), currently placing Estonia among the top 10 countries in the European Union with respect to Internet penetration (Europe Internet Usage 2004) and online availability of public services (Online services 2004).

On the basis of the data presented above, we can conclude that the average TV viewing time in Estonia increased remarkably up to the year 2003 and then stabilised. We can also conclude that the general amount of radio listening has been quite stable, remaining on the same level in 2000-2002, and decreasing only slightly from the year 2003 to 2004.

Radio listening is predominantly (over 90 per cent of the total listening time) a parallel activity to working, driving, talking, eating, etc. As a main activity, it

---

1 As the result of more precise determination of viewing time, the average TV viewing time became shorter. Comparing the data from November 2002 and November 2003, the decrease was 44 minutes (see Table 3). An additional effect was obviously produced by the extended age limits of the sample, as the amount of viewing time among the age groups 4-14 and over 75 is a bit smaller, compared to the average of the previous sample (covering ages from 15 to 74). The fact that the average TV viewing time in November 2004 has not changed compared to the data of November 2003 (4 hours 6 minutes and 4 hours 4 minutes respectively) proves our assumption about the effects of methodology as the reason why the data from 2002 and 2003 are so different.

In 2003, some important changes were also introduced in data collection methodology concerning radio audiences. Since January 2003, the listener's diary has become more precise; respondents are instructed that they should not only mark what radio channel they are listening to, but also where they are doing it – at home, at the workplace, in a car. Table 3 shows that as a result of this change, much more frequent determination of occasional radio listening had taken place, and the average listening time has increased for almost one and a half hours per day. Besides the mentioned change in the diary format, there is no other reason to expect such a big increase in radio listening time, which has been very stable for years.

took up only about 20 minutes per day in the years 1976-1983 (Lõhmus & Vihalemm 2004: 108). Presumably the share of radio listening as a main activity has decreased even more during the last two decades, due to the increasing role of music and entertainment in the content of radio programs.

When analysing press reading in Estonia, a distinction is usually made between two levels of reading – regular and irregular. As empirical indicators of reading regularity we have used answers to the question, "Have you read some of each of the last six issues of this publication?" Reading from at least four of the last six issues has been interpreted as regular reading, one to three issues as irregular reading.[2] In the following analysis we have used indices of regular contacts with newspapers and magazines based on aggregated answers about regularity of reading for all newspapers and respectively also for all magazines.

In Table 3 press reading is characterised by two kinds of aggregated indicators, which are complementary to each other – the share of people who generally and regularly read newspapers, magazines, and other periodicals (according to the above-mentioned criteria, used by the TNS Emor) and the average number of generally and regularly read newspapers and magazines. These indicators highlight slightly different trends in press reading. On the basis of Table 3 we can conclude that the share of newspaper readers among the Estonian adult population was quite stable in 2000-2002 and was slightly decreasing in 2003-2004. Only about 5-10 per cent do not read any newspapers at all, but a much larger number of people, 25-30 per cent, do not read newspapers regularly. As we can see from below, there is also a difference in regular newspaper reading between Estonians and non-Estonians; between the young generation on the one hand, and middle-aged and elderly people on the other. At the same time the average number of newspapers read regularly or irregularly is clearly decreasing.

Comparing the data for the average number of newspapers read by the Estonian population with the circulation figures, we noticed that the average decrease in newspaper circulation that occurred in 1990-1995 was much greater than the decline in newspaper reading (Vihalemm & Juha 2004: 305). We can assume

2 These indicators have been used by the leading Estonian marketing research and consulting company TNS Emor Ltd, presented also in Tables 3 and 4 (general reading = regular + irregular reading).

that one copy of a newspaper was read by more people than in Soviet times, when newspapers were very cheap. People began to read at workplaces and in libraries, to borrow a paper from a neighbour, etc. In recent years the opposite trend can be seen: a clear decline in newspapers reading concurrent with slightly increasing circulation, meaning a decrease in the number of readers per copy.

Compared to newspapers, recent trends in reading magazines and other periodicals are relatively similar, with the exception that the number of periodicals read by the average Estonian decreased in 2004 more than the number of newspapers. Since the year 2000, the interest in magazine reading, initially boosted by a new variety of titles, formats, and topics, started to decrease.

Summarising the time devoted to the daily media use among the adult Estonian population, one can estimate that the length of an average media day is 9 hours 20 minutes. This time is spent overwhelmingly with broadcasting (8 hours and 25 minutes), while the estimated time for press reading and Internet usage is only 55 minutes.

Social Factors of Media Use

The long tradition of media and communication research in Estonia (see Vihalemm 2001) has given us an opportunity to trace how social factors affecting media use have changed throughout the last decades.

According to surveys carried out by the Department of Journalism at Tartu University and by the sociological research group of Estonian Radio and Estonian TV in the 1970s and 1980s, the main differentiating factors of general media use during the Soviet era were education and *ethnicity* (see Lauristin *et al* 1987; Vihalemm 2004). These surveys revealed that in the life of local Russians, press reading and radio listening played a remarkably smaller role. The Russian-speaking population, mainly post-war immigrants, were not associated with local cultural traditions and did not use Estonian language media. Besides a weaker reading tradition, a crucial factor was doubtless the fact that in Estonia there were fewer available Russian-language media channels. At the same time, Estonians had a long tradition of newspaper reading. Estonian newspapers and magazines had been an important part of national integration since the middle of the 19th century, and had also preserved this function under Soviet rule (see Hoyer, Lauk & Vihalemm 1993).

Education had a notable influence on press reading (more highly educated people read more), and a smaller effect on radio listening and TV viewing (people with higher education were less active listeners and viewers).

The indicators of current media use in different demographic groups are presented in Tables 4 and 5. Table 4 characterises general media consumption in the main demographic groups in November 2004 on the basis of the same aggregated indicators used in Table 3. Table 5 presents differences in general media use in comparison with the average of the total population. Data in these tables demonstrate that the average number of regularly read newspapers could be chosen as the most distinctive indicator; in the area of magazine reading this could be the average number of magazines and other periodicals generally read.

On the basis of Tables 4 and 5, we can conclude that ethnicity remains one of the main factors affecting media use. It influences consumption of traditional media more than the Internet. A very strong influence on press reading continues to be education, the role of which has increased over the last decade.

During Soviet times, regular reading of several national and local newspapers was quite common in all social groups. Even very specific cultural publications had a large and democratic audience. Due to the quite limited possibilities for political and economic activities, the cultural press (literary magazines, the cultural weekly) became an important carrier of cultural opposition to the Soviet system. For people deprived of political and economic freedom, reading books, as well as the cultural press performed an important compensatory function (see Vihalemm & Lauristin 1997). With the coming of a free market society, this integrative and compensatory role of the press has diminished. The previous democratic character of the readership of cultural publications has narrowed. Due to rising prices and changing functions of the media, reading quality newspapers has become more limited to elite groups of society. In 1990-2001, the circulation of the cultural weekly dropped 25 fold; circulation of the two leading national dailies 3,5 fold. The share of people with higher education in the audience of the two leading national dailies has increased by 47%, whereas its share in the audience of the

Table 4: Aggregated Indicators of Media Use in Estonia in Main Demographic Groups, November 2004

	Ethnicity			Gender		Age						Education		
	All population	Estonians	Non-Estonians	Men	Women	15-19	20-29	30-39	40-49	50-59	60-74	Primary	Secondary	Higher
Newspaper reading														
General reading (share of readers, %)	90.8	93.5	85.5	88.0	93.3	94.8	88.6	93.8	90.7	90.5	88.7	85.9	91.2	96.2
Regular readers (share of readers, %)	70.5	78.1	55.5	68.9	71.9	54.0	61.1	71.9	75.2	79.5	74.9	60.0	70.6	84.1
Average number of newspapers generally read	3.35	3.54	2.98	3.11	3.58	3.13	3.29	3.64	3.72	3.50	2.81	2.40	3.29	4.77
Average number of newspapers regularly read	1.83	2.09	1.32	1.70	1.94	1.08	1.50	1.83	2.24	2.19	1.87	1.17	1.75	2.94
Reading of magazines and other periodicals														
General reading (share of readers, %)	80.7	85.0	72.0	76.8	84.0	89.6	84.7	86.6	81.0	74.5	71.7	75.5	81.8	83.9
Regular readers (share of readers, %)	63.8	71.7	48.1	58.2	68.7	69.4	60.8	66.9	64.2	61.6	62.3	59.2	63.8	69.8
Average number of periodicals generally read	3.99	5.07	1.84	3.36	4.54	5.55	4.48	4.63	4.07	3.61	2.42	3.41	3.85	5.19
Average number of periodicals regularly read	1.92	2.45	0.88	1.52	2.27	2.23	1.88	2.15	1.97	2.01	1.51	1.55	1.86	2.60
Use of electronic media														
Radio: listening time per day (hours, min)	4: 41	4: 55	4: 13	4: 47	4: 36	3: 53	4: 29	4: 10	4: 44	5: 04	5: 50	4: 18	5: 00	4: 09
Television: viewing time per day (hours, min)	4: 06	4: 02	4: 15	3: 48	4: 21	3: 01	3: 09	3: 45	4: 23	4: 33	5: 34	3: 58	4: 14	4: 03
Internet: have used during last six months (%)	47.4	52.8	36.6	49.7	45.4	88.2	76.2	58.6	45.8	29.7	6.2	37.1	44.0	71.2

* The sample in the case of press reading and Internet usage represent population aged 15-74; for TV viewing, the population older than 4 years; for radio listening population aged 12-74.

Source: TNS Emor Ltd.

Table 5: Differences in Media Use by Main Demographic Groups, November 2004

(Average of all Population = 100)

	Ethnicity			Gender		Age						Education		
	All population	Estonians	Non-Estonians	Men	Women	15-19	20-29	30-39	40-49	50-59	60-74	Primary	Secondary	Higher
Newspaper reading														
General reading (share of readers)	100	103	94	97	103	104	98	97	100	100	98	95	100	106
Regular reading (share of readers)	100	111	79	98	102	77	87	102	107	113	106	85	100	119
Average number of newspapers generally read	100	106	89	93	106	93	98	109	111	104	84	72	98	142
Average number of newspapers regularly read	100	114	72	93	106	59	82	100	122	120	102	74	94	161
Reading of magazines and other periodicals														
General reading (share of readers)	100	105	89	95	104	111	105	107	100	92	89	94	101	104
Regular reading (share of readers)	100	112	75	91	108	109	95	105	101	97	98	93	100	109
Average number of periodicals generally read	100	127	46	84	114	139	113	116	102	90	61	85	96	130
Average number of periodicals regularly read	100	128	46	79	118	116	98	112	103	105	79	81	97	135
Use of electronic media														
Radio: listening time per day	100	105	91	102	98	83	96	89	101	108	125	92	107	89
Television: viewing time per day	100	98	104	93	106	74	77	91	107	110	136	97	103	99
Internet: have used during last six months	100	111	77	105	96	186	161	124	97	63	13	78	93	150

Source: TNS Emor Ltd.

cultural weekly has even grown 2.3 fold (Vihalemm & Kõuts 2004: 74; Vihalemm & Juha 2004: 307, 339).

Age has become a new and very important factor impacting general media use. Large disparities between the age groups appear not only in Internet usage but also in newspaper and magazine reading, radio listening, and TV viewing. The youngest group (aged 15-19) makes more frequent use of the Internet than the second group (aged 20-29), and for multiple purposes: entertainment, reading newspapers and magazines, listening to music and following RV and radio programs, studying and communicating with friends (Vengerfeldt & Runnel 2004). This trend indicates the beginning of a fundamental shift in media usage in Estonia: among the youngest age group we can speak about an Internet-centred media environment and, as a matter of fact, about media convergence.

Comparing the patterns of general media use in different age groups (Figure 1), one can see that the Estonian young generation is clearly oriented to the Internet and reads significantly more general-interest magazines, whereas the older generation is oriented to TV viewing and radio listening.

Figure 1: Patterns of Media Use in Different Age Groups (Percentage of Difference from Average Level in November 2004)

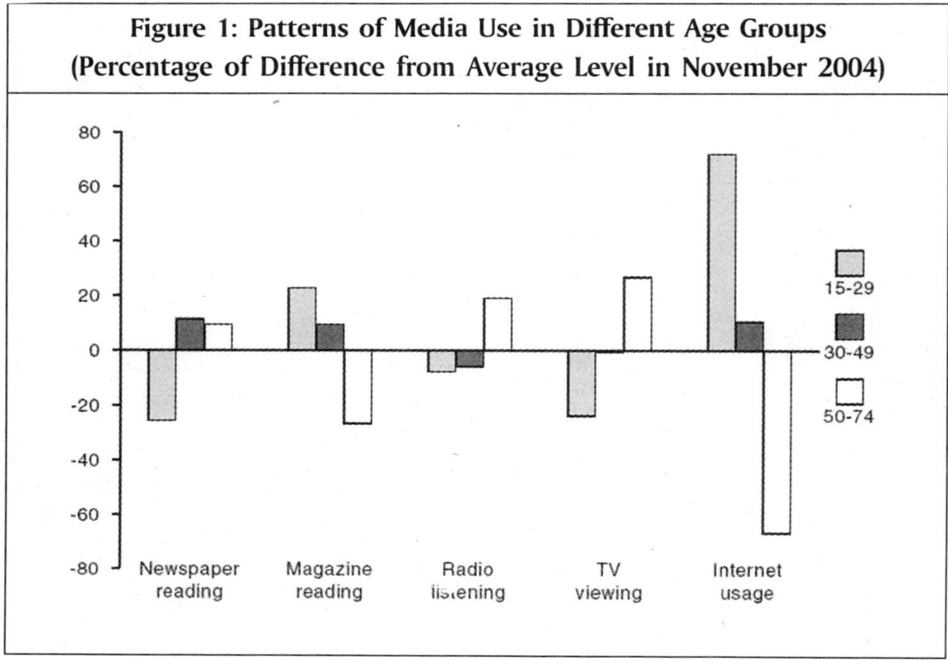

It is important to mention that even if the young generation demonstrates the same level of newspaper reading, there is a larger share of irregular readers among them, who perhaps browse through the content of newspapers via the Internet. This is a characteristic feature of their newspaper reading, but not of magazine reading.

Comparison of Media Use Trends in Estonia, Finland and Sweden

The recent changes in media use by Estonians seem quite dramatic, compared to the relatively stable picture of media use in the Nordic countries. Media use volume in Sweden has been quite stable over decades – average time for radio listening was 133 minutes per day as in 1986 as well in 1999, for TV viewing respectively 100 and 98 minutes, for newspaper reading 34 minutes and 28 minutes (Nordicom-Sveriges Medie-barometer 2003: 21). Although radio and TV trends in Finland over 1986-1999 have been relatively similar to Estonia (average radio listening time has grown by 31% and TV viewing time by 59%), newspaper reading (average newspaper reading time) has also been quite stable in Finland across the three decades 1971-2000, with a very slight decrease in the mid-1990s (see Wiio & Nordenstreng 2003: 14).

The average media day of Estonian users is longer than in the Nordic countries: approximately an hour longer than in Finland (8 hours and 14 minutes in 2002 according to World Press Trends 2003)[3] and about two hours longer than in Norway and Denmark, but over four hours longer than in Sweden. Media use in Estonia can be characterised by very active radio listening and TV viewing. Only in Ireland is the average listening time longer than in Estonia (World Press Trends 2003: 149); the average TV viewing in 2002 was exceeded only by Macedonia, the USA, and Hungary (Television 2003 – International Key Facts). The very approximate figure of time spent in Estonia on reading printed media and using Internet seems quite comparable with the Nordic countries: in Finland in 2002 it was 1 hour and 34 minutes (World Press Trends 2003: 116); in Sweden in 2003, 1 hour and 8 minutes (Nordicom-Sveriges Mediebarometer 2003: 23); in Germany in 2003, 1 hour 2 minutes (World Press Trends 2004: 155).

[3] These data contradict the data of the Intermedia research conducted by Finnish Gallup in 2002 – according to them the average media day in Finland was 9 hours and 22 minutes, quite similarly to Estonia (Wiio & Nordenstreng 2003: 15).

Comparing our data about the age groups with the data showing the average time spent in 2003 on different media channels in Sweden, one can see similar trends in newspaper reading and radio listening in both countries: young people are reading newspapers less and listening less to the radio (time spent in Sweden on reading dailies in age group 15-24 was 53% from an average of the whole population, that of radio listening 74% respectively). However, Swedish youth watches more TV and reads fewer magazines than average: time spent on watching TV was 107% compared to the average, and 67% spent on magazine reading. Internet usage is more similar between the age groups in Sweden than in Estonia, although the oldest age group 65-79 differs greatly from the average (Nordicom-Sveriges Mediebarometer 2003: 23).

Comparison of the data concerning the average time spent on different media in Finland (Finnish Mass Media 2004) shows quite similar trends with Sweden with respect to radio listening, but not for magazine reading and TV viewing. In Finland there are no differences between age groups in average time for magazine reading (Finnish Mass Media 2004: 222). Similarly to Estonia the young generation is spending much less time on TV viewing, compared to middle aged and older people. In all three countries young people are less active newspaper readers, compared to the other age groups (Table 6).

Table 6: Comparison of Traditional Media Use by Age Groups in Three Countries (Average of adult population in respective country = 100)

	Estonia 2004			Sweden 2003			Finland 2002-04*		
	15-19	40-59	60-74	15-24	45-64	65-79	15-24	45-64	65-
Newspaper reading**	59	121	102	53	120	170	52	127	165
Magazine reading**	116	104	79	67	113	153	97	97	106
Radio Listening***	83	104	125	74	116	121	68	121	130
TV viewing***	74	108	136	107	98	124	61	116	153

* Press reading data are based on a slightly different age classification: 12-24, 45-59, and over 60

** In Sweden and Finland, average reading time per day; in Estonia, the number of regularly read newspapers/magazines and other periodicals

** * Average listening and viewing time per day.

Sources: TNS Emor, Nordicom-Sveriges Mediebarometer 2003, Finnish Mass Media 2004.

The most active newspaper readers in Finland as in Sweden are older people, while in Estonia the most active press readers are middle-aged people (age 40-59). It seems that the common trend, aging of the newspaper readership, began among Estonian readership later, only after the 1990s, while in the Nordic countries this tendency emerged already in the middle of the 1980s.

On the basis of the data about the daily reach of newspapers in age groups it can also be concluded that in many other countries (France, Germany, the USA) there is a trend toward more occasional newspaper reading among young people, compared to the middle aged and especially the older generation. There are some exceptions, however, for example, Norway, the UK, Lithuania (World Press Trends 2004). The regularity of newspaper reading among young people in Finland decreased significantly in the years 1985-1999, but has stabilised at the beginning of the new century (Hujanen 2002). In Estonia there has been much discussion concerning the aging of newspaper readers and possible strategies for bringing back younger readers.

Concluding Remarks

1. The patterns of general media use in the main demographic groups clearly demonstrate differences, not only in use of the new media but also in use of traditional media. This allows us to argue that we should speak about a media divide, not only about a digital divide (see Vihalemm & Lauristin 2002).
2. General media use in Estonia during the recent years can be characterised by the increasing importance of the electronic media. This means not only a rapid increase in Internet usage (by 2004 the share of Internet users had reached half of the Estonian population), but also a marked increase in time spent on TV watching. Both trends are common for all European countries. However, growth in TV watching has been dramatic – not only in Estonia as compared to Nordic countries, but as a trend typical of all post-communist societies. This is probably connected with a greater need for relaxation, caused by rapid transformation in all spheres of life, and by a turn to the more intensive and demanding situation of permanent competition.

3. Among the social factors of media use, ethnicity, education, and age are of the greatest general importance. The majority of Estonian Russians are oriented to Russian media (particularly TV); their traditions of press reading and radio listening are weaker compared to Estonians. For younger people, the Internet is of much greater importance. The younger generation is also more entertainment-oriented, reading fewer newspapers and more general interest magazines compared to middle-aged and older people, and preferring commercial radio and TV channels to the public ones.
4. The uses of traditional and new media are in general complementary to each other. Only in the youngest group (aged 15-19) can we observe that with the Internet becoming a multifunctional channel, the use of traditional media (particularly TV) is on the decrease. In a significant group of people (21 per cent of all respondents) the Internet and interpersonal communication at the workplace or in school were evaluated as much more important sources for news and knowledge than TV newscasts, which were clearly leading sources for the majority of the population.
5. The main problem with international comparisons is the lack of comparable data on media systems and especially on media use. In situations where the data about media use in different countries are based on different indicators and different methodology, cross-national comparisons could be made using differences drawn from the average of the total population, and measured by the particular set of indicators in the each country.
6. There is a need for an international agreement concerning key indicators in the field of media and for an agreement on the harmonisation of methodology and criteria of data gathering. Such an agreement should be made on the basis of international discussion among researchers, and initiated by the EU institutions.

(Peeter Vihalemm, Professor, Department of Journalism and Communication, University of Tartu, Ülikooli 18, EE- Tartu 50090. The author can be reached at peeter.vihalemm@ut.ee).

References

Emor 2004 – The number of Internet users in Estonia has exceeded 600 000. Emor news archive 22.06.2004. *www.emor.ee/eng/arhiiv.html?keyword=31*

Europe Internet Usage 2004 – Europe Internet Usage Stats and 2004 Population Statistics. *www.internetworldstats.com/stats4.htm*

Finnish Mass Media 2002, 2004. Helsinki: Statistics Finland.

Hasebrink, Uwe & Anja Herzog (2004) Mediennutzung im internationalen Vergleich. In Christiane Matzen & Anja Herzog (ed) *Internationale Handbuch Medien 2004/2005*. Baden-Baden: Nomos.

Herron, Erik (1999) Democratization and the Development of Information Regimes: The Internet in Eurasia and in the Baltics. *Problems of Post-Communism*, 46, 6, 56-68.

Høyer, Svennik; Epp Lauk & Peeter Vihalemm (eds) (1993) *Towards a Civic Society: The Baltic Media's Long Road to Freedom*. Tartu: Baltic Association for Media Research/Nota Baltica Ltd.

Hujanen, Erkki (2002) Sanomalehtien tilaamattomuus. In *Finnish Mass Media 2002*. Helsinki: Statistics Finland.

Lauk, Epp (1996) Estonian Journalists in Search of New Professional Identity. *Javnost/The Public*, 3, 4, 93-106.

Lauk, Epp (1997) *Historical and Sociological Perspectives on the Development of Estonian Journalism*. Dissertationes de mediis et communicationibus Universitatis Tartuensis 1. Tartu: Tartu University Press.

Lauk, Epp & Halliki Harro (2003) A Landscape After the Storm: Development of the Estonian Media in the 1990s. In David Paletz & Karol Jakubowicz (eds) *Business as Usual: Continuity and Change in Central and Eastern European Media*. Creskill, NJ: Hampton Press.

Lauristin, Marju (1998) Transformations of Public Sphere and Changing Role of the Media in Post-Communist Society. In Piotr Sztompka (ed.) *Building Open Society and Perspectives of Sociology in East-Central Europe*. Pre-Congress Volumes of the 14th World Congress of Sociology. Montreal: International Sociological Association.

Lauristin, Marju; Peeter Vihalemm; Sulev Uus & Juhan Peegel (1987) *Rajoonileht ja lugeja* [Local paper and its reader]. Tallinn: Eesti Raamat.

Lauristin, Marju & Vihalemm, Peeter (1993) The Awakening. In Svennik Høyer; Epp Lauk & Peeter Vihalemm (eds) (1993) *Towards a Civic Society: The Baltic Media's Long Road to Freedom*. Tartu: Baltic Association for Media Research/Nota Baltica Ltd.

Lauristin, Marju & Peeter Vihalemm (1998) Media Use and Social Changes in Estonia. In *Estonian Human Development Report 1998.* Tallinn: UNDP. Available electronically – *www.iiss.ee/nhdr/1998/ EIA98eng.pdf*

Lauristin, Marju & Peeter Vihalemm (2002) The Transformation of Estonian Society and Media: 1987-2001. In Peeter Vihalemm (ed) *Baltic Media in Transition.* Tartu: Tartu University Press.

Lõhmus, Maarja & Peeter Vihalemm (2004) Raadio Eestis 1960-2004: struktuur, programm ja kuulajad (Radio in Estonia in 1960-2004: structure, programme and listeners). In Peeter Vihalemm (ed) *Meediasüsteem ja meediakasutus Eestis 1965-2004.* Tartu: Tartu Ülikooli Kirjastus.

Nordicom-Sveriges Mediebarometer 2003. *MedieNotiser* 1, 2004. Göteborg: Nordicom-Sverige & Göte-borgs universitet.

Online services 2004 – Online Availability of Public Services: How is Europe Progressing? Report of the Fifth Measurement, October 2004. *http://europa.eu.int/information_society/soccul/egov/egov_ benchmarking_2005.pdf*

Paulson, Tiiu (1986) Auditooriumist [About audience]. In *ENSV Teleraadiokomitee panoraam 1985.* Tallinn: Eesti Raamat.

Paulson, Tiiu (1993) Eesti NSVst Eesti Vabariiki. Käsikiri (From ESSR to Estonian Republic. Mimeo). Tallinn: Telirad.

Saar, Andrus (1985) TV ja raadio auditooriumi uurimise tulemusi [Results of broadcasting audience research]. In *ENSV Teleraadiokomitee panoraam 1984.* Tallinn: Eesti Raamat.

Tapinas, Laimonas (1998) The Print Media. In Helga Schmid (ed.) *Understanding the Media in the Baltic States.* Düsseldorf: European Institute for the Media.

Television 2003 – International Key Facts (2003) Köln: RTL Group & IP International Marketing Committee.

Vengerfeldt, Pille & Pille Runnel (2004) Uus meedia Eestis [New media in Estonia]. In Peeter Vihalemm (ed) *Meediasüsteem ja meediakasutus Eestis 1965-2004.* Tartu: Tartu Ülikooli Kirjastus.

Vihalemm, Peeter (2001) Development of Media Research in Estonia. *Nordicom Review,* 22, 2, 79-92.

Vihalemm, Peeter (ed) *Meediasüsteem ja meediakasutus Eestis 1965-2004* (Media system and media use in Estonia in 1965-2004). Tartu: Tartu Ülikooli Kirjastus.

Vihalemm Peeter; Epp Lauk & Marju Lauristin (1997) Estonian Media in the Process of Change. In Marju Lauristin & Peeter Vihalemm with Karl Erik Rosengren & Lennart Weibull (eds)

Return to the Western World: Cultural and Political Perspectives on Estonian Post-Communist Transition. Tartu: Tartu University Press.

Vihalemm, Peeter & Marju Lauristin (1997) Political Control and Ideological Canonisation. The Estonian Press during the Soviet Period. In Eduard Mühle (ed) *Vom Instrument der Partei zur "vierten Gewalt".* Marburg: Herder-Institut.

Vihalemm, Peeter & Marju Lauristin (2002) Indicators of Media Development in Estonia. In *Defining 'Key Indicators' in the Field of Media and Communication Research in Europe. Conference Papers.* Dortmund : University of Dortmund.

Vihalemm, Peeter & Leie Juha (2004) Trükisõna ja lugejad (Printed media and readers). In Peeter Vihalemm (ed), *Meediasüsteem ja meediakasutus Eestis 1965-2004.* Tartu: Tartu Ülikooli Kirjastus.

Vihalemm, Peeter & Ragne Kõuts (2004) Trükisõna ja lugejaskond Eestis 1965-2004 (Printed media and its audience in Estonia in 1965-2004). In Peeter Vihalemm (ed) *Meediasüsteem ja meediakasutus Eestis 1965-2004.* Tartu: Tartu Ülikooli Kirjastus.

Vihalemm, Triin (1999) Local and Global Orientations of Media Consumption in Estonia. In *Estonian Human Development Report 1999.* Tallinn: UNDP. Available electronically – *www.iiss.ee/nhdr/1999/EIA99eng.pdf*

Wiio, Osmo & Kaarle Nordenstreng, Kaarle (2003) Viestintäjärjelstelmä. In Kaarle Nordenstreng & Osmo Wiio (ed) *Suomen mediamaisema.* 2. painos. Vantaa: WSOY.

World Press Trends 2003 (2004). Paris: World Association of Newspapers & Zenithmedia.

Index